Gentle Femdom Diaries

Interviews with Real Kinksters

Gentle Femdom Diaries

Interviews with Real Kinksters

M Kay Noir

CONTENT WARNING

This book is intended for a mature audience only. It contains educational discussions around sexual and mental health themes.

Trigger Warning (TW): Be advised that some interviews include mention of suicidal thoughts and mental health struggles. Abuse is also mentioned.

If at any point this book makes you feel unsafe, please stop reading.

CONTENTS

For anyone with desires deemed "unconventional" by society, may you find validation in these conversations around healthy kink dynamics.

DISCLAIMER

The views and opinions expressed in the following work do not reflect the views of the author. They are the personal views of each person interviewed.

Every interview was approved by the person (or people) interviewed and written consent was obtained to publish this work. The stories have been put together by reworking the actual audio interview transcripts.

The information contained within this book is strictly for educational purposes. If you wish to apply the ideas shared in this book, you are taking full responsibility for your actions. This book is not intended to be a substitute for any professional advice. It merely aims to share the insights contained in the interviews conducted.

The author has made every effort to ensure the accuracy of the information within this book at the time of publication. The author does not assume and hereby disclaims any liability to any party for any loss, damage, or disruption caused by errors or omissions, whether such errors or omissions result from accident, negligence, or any other cause.

WHAT IS GENTLE FEMDOM?

The official definition, according to *Urban Dictionary*, is as follows:

"A subset of the femdom family of kinks that emerged in rejection of (what was perceived to be) an unrealistically male-centered, violent, and unsentimental kind of femdom content that is popular on mainstream porn sites."

How I interpret this is:

Easy on the mind, rough on the body (consensually).

Consent, communication, and trust are the pillars of a beautiful, kinky life. But make no mistake—just because it's "gentle" on your mental health, does not mean you will not end up bruised and bound (if that is what you want).

The gentle part refers to your mind, not your body. You can still be in a gentle femdom relationship and enjoy impact play, for instance.

It is about negotiating and respecting boundaries, about looking after each other, and creating a healthy relationship where all parties' needs are being met.

FOREWORD

When I started researching femdom to inform my erotic romance books, I was bombarded by mostly toxic representations online. All I saw was abusive tendencies and male-gaze fantasies portrayed as absolute reality. Just scantily clothed women with whips telling men to "do as I say" with no regard for anyone's safety or mental health.

(Not that there is anything wrong with a scantily clothed woman hurling a whip around. As long as there is consent involved and all parties' needs are considered. But my concern was the lack of representation around safe and responsible kink.)

As my community on social media grew, so did the number of people who reached out to me to discuss their desires and dynamics. Sure, a lot of these interactions were simply unsolicited pictures and rude messages, but some were genuine messages from loving, kind, and supportive people who believed in safe spaces and healthy kink relationships.

My interactions with the Dommes were far more encouraging than those with the cis heterosexual men who could not get beyond the social construct of gender roles (*not all of them, of course*). The Dommes were so gentle, so wise. They were just everyday people you would meet at the office, or in the supermarket, maybe at a friend's dinner party...Just everyday people who were tired of being represented as abusive or mentally ill simply for enjoying kinky play.

An idea started brewing. I wanted to show the different side of femdom dynamics. I wanted to tell the love stories of those who have found supportive partners who care for each other. (*Sure, they might enjoy beating the sh*t out of each other sometimes, but they truly care about their partner's well-being.*) What does it *really* take to be in a gentle femdom dynamic?

On the other hand, I also wanted to educate those who seemed lost. Those who saw an image or read a story—maybe watched a porno—and saw something that spoke to their desires. But then only found confusing representation down the line, if any. How could they find what they're looking for? What should they do (or not do) to increase their chances of finding a suitable partner?

I decided to put my journalism skills to good use and speak to *real* kinky people to find out what their lives are like. After nearly 20 years of working as a professional trade journalist and magazine editor, it was time to shift focus to a topic I was even more curious about. Interviewing and telling stories have always been my strong points. It was time to delve into BDSM journalism.

It was December 2022 when I finally mustered the courage to approach **Miss Kitty** on Instagram. She had been replying to some of my posts with great educational points and seemed open to discussions.

I expected to be shot down but Miss Kitty saw the value of what I was trying to do. As usual, I over-explained myself, my vision, carefully laying out the questions for pre-approval and assuring her that we could absolutely skip anything she was not comfortable discussing. We arranged to meet via a Zoom audio-only call.

We chatted away longer than I initially planned. Miss Kitty was so open and so sweet, I really learned a lot from her—especially about responsible kink.

The response to the article was incredible. From Day 1, across all platforms, the hunger for real information was clear. After every interview, I was convinced it would be the last, that nobody would ever be willing to chat with a complete stranger about their most private sex life. But every time I was pleasantly surprised.

Never more so than my interview with **Venus**, the second in the series. What an inspiration! She really made it all fall into place for me and made me realize what content I wanted to create and for which audience. She was just someone I could imagine myself being friends with in real life (*maybe if we lived closer*).

I left every interview so energized. Slowly, the series grew as more women spoke up about taking charge of their own pleasure and finding joy in gentle femdom. They showed me, in so many different ways, how kink relationships can be beautiful. Women from all over the world, finding their inner Domme and learning to love themselves. Dommes from the United States (US), Australia, the United Kingdom (UK), and even as far as Thailand—proving that you do not have to be mean to be dominant.

Madam Mayhem gave me a glimpse into the world of Pro-Dommes too, and really impressed me with her kind and caring approach. She showed me that age truly is just a number and it is never too late to discover yourself and upgrade your pleasure.

Goddess Pinky was just a bundle of energy. She shared her amazing journey of being a submissive herself and learning to be a Domme. We spoke for way too long. It ended up being a 32-page interview transcript. What a joy!

Miss Liya gave me insight into a younger generation and how sometimes dominance can be completely natural. It does not have to be stuck in boxes with labels. She made it all seem so beautifully effortless.

Goddess Beatriz made me rethink my idea of what a Domme is and showed me that everyone is truly unique, a real person with real likes and wants, not just a kink dispenser for male fantasies.

The final interview was with the lovely couple, **Queen Nazz and Ari**. It was so sweet interviewing them together, despite our 12-hour time-zone difference. Their relationship is so fun and lighthearted; I could really feel their amazing energy.

Every single one of these interviews has been read and approved by the people interviewed. I will always be incredibly grateful to them for trusting me with their stories and allowing me to publish this resource. Representation matters.

I hope you learn as much from these incredible people as I did. May some of your questions find answers and if not, may you learn how to ask in a respectful way.

In summary, stay kinky, stay kind.
Consent first—always.

M KAY NOIR

INTERVIEWS

WHEN MISS KITTY MET HER PIGGY, A LOVE STORY

Bisexual British Domme Miss Kitty openly talks about her BDSM journey, mental health challenges, and finding a new submissive after her divorce. What does a real-life female-led, kinky relationship look like? The short answer—it looks nothing like it does in porn.

Miss Kitty (36) and her "special boy," Piggy (40), are based in the UK. They met online three years ago and now live together as a BDSM dynamic, practicing a kinky Female Domination (Femdom) lifestyle.

After more than a decade in the BDSM community, Miss Kitty's key message is that being a Domme is a huge responsibility—do not take it lightly. And to subs: try and be more careful and less desperate.

Here follows the couple's uncensored story, as told by Miss Kitty with the full informed consent of her partner.

Getting into Kink

Miss Kitty initially got into BDSM when she was 19—more than 17 years ago now. Finding this community was "sheer fluke," she explains. A new partner's friends, who were a little older than her, were practicing BDSM and brought the topic into general conversation. This got the young couple curious and they decided to start experimenting with kink themselves.

At first, Miss Kitty played the submissive—a more conventional role for a female. However, she quickly found that it was not in her nature to be submissive. Whenever her partner would dominate her, she kept thinking that she could do it better than him. "And then I realized, actually, I'm not submissive at all."

Miss Kitty views that experience as helpful to her life as Domme, allowing her to better understand what it feels like to relinquish some level of control.

Luckily for Miss Kitty, her partner at the time was discovering that he was a bit of a Switch (someone who enjoys both dominant and submissive roles), and he was happy to let her take control from time to time. The couple continued their journey of exploration and discovery until splitting up about a year later.

Miss Kitty did not get into any new exclusive dynamics after that. Instead, she enjoyed multiple play-partners, or as she affectionately calls them—"fuck buddies." These were "like a kinky hook-up, but with a defined dynamic." It was not just about the sexual experience though. Miss Kitty still spoke to these partners outside of the dynamic as well, regularly checking in with them as human beings too—not just about kinky stuff.

Finding New Play-Partners

It can be a desperate matter for many to find suitable BDSM play partners in real life. Miss Kitty generally found them at her local heavy metal goth nightclub. She described it as a place for all the "weirdos" (including herself) to come together, making it a bit easier to broach the often-taboo topic of BDSM.

After a few drinks, once people were generally more open, Miss Kitty would jokingly slip some kinky comments into the conversation. Often, people would laugh it off at the time, but the seed was planted. Then later, she would get a text from the person about her comment, curious about kink.

Even at her work where they had a close-knit team, sometimes some joking, off-the-cuff comments would lead to new play-partners.

Trying a Vanilla Life

After living this way for the better part of a decade, Miss

Kitty decided she needed a more stable life. At the time, she was going through a rough patch in her personal life and had just been diagnosed with bipolar disorder.

While Miss Kitty was in recovery for a severe bipolar episode, she met the man who would become her husband (and later ex-husband). "I was going through a bit of a personal identity crisis," she explains. "I had this concept in my brain that I just want to be a normal person; I just want to fit in and have a normal life." He was the answer to that need for a "normal" life.

They got married. He had a child from a previous relationship and Miss Kitty stepped up as the stepmom. "It gave me the little secure family unit I thought I wanted," she says. "At that time, I did need that stability. But as I became more comfortable and confident in myself and accepting of my illness, I actually started realizing that I was trying to fit in a mold that wasn't for me."

Her husband was not into kinky stuff at all. Miss Kitty remembers subtly dropping hints about pegging but he was having none of it, saying it would "never" happen. After a while, it became clear that they did not really have that much in common. Once Miss Kitty stopped trying to fit in and started being more herself, their differences started pushing a wedge between them and they drifted apart.

After three years, they got divorced. They are still on good terms and things did not get ugly, but they just realized that they wanted different things.

An Unconventional Meeting

After the end of her marriage, Miss Kitty was not looking for another partner. She wanted to spend time getting comfortable with herself and gain some of her independence back. Little did she know that the world had other plans, and someone special was waiting just around the corner—as they often are.

Miss Kitty describes the way she met her current partner as "obscure." She did not go looking for anyone. No, she was simply playing an interior decorating mobile game where you could gain extra points if you engaged with other players. Not kinky at all. She did not really want to talk to anyone else that day, she remembers, but needed points to buy a new wallpaper for her house in the game.

As she was strolling around in the game, Miss Kitty saw an avatar with the handle "Slave Pig." She often saw such users online but usually ignored them. On this particular day though, she decided to humor this person and asked them about their interesting name. This opened the conversation with the person who would eventually become her current partner, her "special boy"— her "Piggy."

Training a New Sub

Piggy immediately started calling her "Miss," but Kitty was having none of it. She told him not to call her by a title, but Piggy argued that it was respectful. "No, it's respectful when you are my submissive, which you are not," she told him. "So, you can just talk to me like a normal person." (*Good advice—take note*.)

Piggy, who is also autistic, admitted that he was new to the BDSM scene; that he had fantasized about it for a long time but had zero experience. Miss Kitty found his honesty "refreshing" after encountering so many fake people online projecting experience while having none.

He was keen to learn, and Miss Kitty helped him understand the basics. It quickly became apparent that Piggy wanted a dynamic. But Miss Kitty insisted on talking face-to-face first, even if it was on a video call—"not to perform for me or get his penis out, simply to say hi."

"A lot of the red flags with the online stuff is that often people want these dynamics, but they don't want that connection—it's all fantasy," Miss Kitty explains. "And if I'm going to be putting somebody in a submissive role, I need to know enough about that person to know I can protect them in that submissive space. I don't think you can do that without visual contact, whether that be on video or in person."

Still, Piggy wanted to go straight into a submissive role without any face-to-face interactions because he found it difficult because of his autism, Miss Kitty explains. After discussing this at length, they came up with an alternative solution that would accommodate Piggy's needs too. Miss Kitty helped him through the initial discussion around limits and safe words on a telephone call before meeting, which was more comfortable for Piggy.

The couple-to-be lived a three-hour drive apart. After two weeks of talking, it was finally time to meet in person. Piggy booked a hotel room near Miss Kitty's place for them to meet up and have a play session. It was important for Miss Kitty to meet in real life to see if they had chemistry and whether the dynamic would meet both of their needs. Boundaries are very important to her and she wanted to ensure the relationship would be healthy for both.

They hit it off and Piggy realized his dream of becoming Miss Kitty's collared sub. Despite the distance, they started meeting up a few times a month for kinky play dates and Miss Kitty found herself falling for Piggy. "Through him being just his little charming self, I just fell in love with him," she says. "I just couldn't help myself, despite me trying not to."

————————◇————————

"There is more to being a Dom/me than just having sex and giving orders."
-Miss Kitty

————————◇————————

Navigating Mental Illness

There is more to being a Dom/me than just having sex and giving orders, Miss Kitty advises. "As the dominant, you are the caretaker of that person [your submissive] and their emotional health and well-being within that dynamic. You are taking that on and that is quite a heavy responsibility if you're not prepared for it."

In Piggy's case, this was a huge responsibility, because he was mentally unwell but masking it, Miss Kitty explains. In the early days of their dynamic, he was seeking out high-risk, extreme kink activities—a lot of heavy-impact play and sharp verbal humiliation. "It was almost like he was seeking a punishment. It was almost feeding a self-harm narrative." This raised a big red flag for Miss Kitty.

One day, Piggy unexpectedly broke down in tears during a play session. After uttering his safe words ("too much"), Miss Kitty immediately stopped the scene. Later, during a debriefing session, it became apparent that Piggy had not been able to cry or be vulnerable in front of anyone for many years.

In that moment of play, the emotional walls had come down and it all spilled out. "It was like opening Pandora's Box, which was very, very cathartic for him and added a lot of benefits for him. But as a Domme, I needed to be able to contain that. I needed to be able to nurture him while he was in that very vulnerable place. And sort of help him piece that back together."

Had Miss Kitty not been there in person to contain the situation and support her sub, it could have been very dangerous for Piggy. That is why Miss Kitty cautions against online dynamics where the sub (or Dom/me) is not properly supported. There is much more to a Domme/sub (D/s) dynamic than what you see in pornography, Miss Kitty explains. "You have to be prepared for what happens when you open that door."

At the time, the couple was still traveling back and forth, seeing each other maybe two or three times a month. In between, they kept in touch over video calls and texts, chatting about normal things too, not just kink.

In the summer of 2021, Piggy was overcome with "psychotic depression," as Miss Kitty explains. He had a lot of suicidal thoughts and was very isolated where he lived. Miss Kitty was concerned about some of the things he was saying on the phone. So, she drove over and bundled Piggy and his cats into her car to take him home with her.

Miss Kitty moved him in temporarily, to care for him while he was a risk to himself. By the time Piggy stabilized, it no longer made sense for him to go back. So, he stayed. They have lived together ever since.

Living a Kinky Life

To the average person, Miss Kitty and Piggy seem like any other couple—maybe just a bit eccentric. Their dynamic is known by some close friends, but Miss Kitty's parents, who live next door, have no idea about their kinky lifestyle.

Despite living together, Miss Kitty and Piggy do not practice their dynamic 24/7. "Everybody's different. But for me, sustaining a dominant headspace full-time takes a lot of mental energy," Miss Kitty explains. "It's very intense and tiring." Instead, it sits in the back of her mind during daily functioning, ready to be called on as need be.

"It's easy for him to drop straight into a submissive space, because of his mental health and self-esteem issues," Miss Kitty explains. "And I can default to a dominant role easily. But on a day-to-day basis, I don't think that is healthy." Instead, most of the time they just have normal conversations like any couple without any power imbalances. Especially when it comes to big decisions that affect finances and the household.

"If I know it's a power imbalance in that aspect, I acknowledge it and try and almost coach him to be more equal, if it's relevant. It doesn't feel right for me to abuse the dominant dynamic to have things my way. I'm more of a soft dominant these days."

Although their dynamic includes a lot of nurturing and mothering ("sweet with a hint of patronizing" Miss Kitty calls it), the couple does not practice age play—like Mommy-Domme-little-boy (MDlb) scenes often seen online. It is simply not their thing. "That's the thing with BDSM—your dynamic is unique to you two," she explains. It's important to ensure both parties' needs are met in the dynamic.

The Danger of Online

When Miss Kitty and Piggy first started their dynamic, the sub-to-be had a lot of unrealistic ideas based on what he had seen online. Miss Kitty recalls the story of Piggy's first pegging. Although he had never tried it before, he was very eager to, based on what he had seen in porn. So, Miss Kitty sent her special boy off to buy a dildo in a size he thought would be appropriate. He came back with a 9-inch "monster."

Miss Kitty explained that he was being a bit ambitious, but Piggy insisted he could take it. That is when Miss Kitty took the executive decision, as the more experienced partner, to not use that dildo. If she did, there was a risk that Piggy could come to physical harm—no matter how much lube she used. Instead, Miss Kitty made him get rid of it and acquired a more suitable-sized toy. After the first occurrence, Piggy quickly realized that the big dildo would never have worked.

According to Miss Kitty, that is the biggest danger with online representation—the unsafe extremes. "It's dangerous because it makes it look like anybody could do it with the right mindset." Yet there is little to no representation of how to do things safely.

Miss Kitty's hard limits are based on what could be physically dangerous to a person. As she works in a healthcare setting, she has seen the damage of unsafe play first-hand. "Obviously, there are safe ways to do it and people do, but that's not a responsibility I want to take on," she explains. "Because, even if I do it safely, that person can still go home and try and recreate it themselves, potentially causing damage." That is why her limits include things like urethral sounding and anal fisting.

Another extreme that she does not get involved in is ball-busting and intense cock-and-ball torture

(CBT)—something very common in extreme porn but less so in real-life gentle femdom dynamics. "It's sort of glamorized in extreme hardcore BDSM porn but the risk isn't highlighted. A lot of subs, especially those new to BDSM, almost have this preconceived idea that a good sub does as they're told, and a good sub will take what's given to them. That's where the danger comes in." Important note: You do not have to do things you are not comfortable with to be a "good sub."

"A sub actually carries more control than the dominant...the sub has a safe word, giving them ultimate control."
-Miss Kitty

Too Many Fakes

Miss Kitty cautions against people pretending to be dominant online—those gaslighting submissives into crossing their own boundaries and not respecting the idea of consent.

"A sub actually carries more control than the dominant," Miss Kitty explains. "As a Domme, I judge my sub's limits and what they're willing to do or not do. But at the end of the day, no matter how extreme you get, the sub has a safe word, giving them ultimate control. If a Dom/me says you don't need a safe word, get away from that person—it's a massive red flag. If they are trying to guilt you or manipulate you into doing something you genuinely don't want to do, and you've communicated why you don't want to, then they are not a genuine Dom/me."

"BDSM is not an excuse to be a bad person. Coercive control is a form of domestic abuse," Miss Kitty says. "Often people try and wrap a bow on controlling, manipulative behavior and call it BSDM. But it's not BDSM, you're just a bad partner—no matter what type of relationship you enter."

"A good Domme, whether you are just a play-partner or in a loving relationship with that person, is protective over your submissive," according to Miss Kitty. "A good dominant will support their submissive to be able to be themself; you will embrace them as their individual self. They might be a submissive version of themselves, but they should feel comfortable being there and being vulnerable. And you can't expect them to feel safe if you are bullying someone into a vulnerable position."

Advice for New Submissives

Miss Kitty advises subs to trust their instincts. "If something's giving you a red flag, it's a red flag. Even if the person you're talking to is genuine, if it's giving you a red flag, that means that person isn't the right play partner for you."

Finding the right play partner can be very difficult, especially if you are shy and reserved. That is why a lot of people prefer to dip their toe into online stuff first—they do not want to expose themselves as a kinkster in real life. The issue comes when the people they are trying to find are in the same position. It is easy for people to want to "fake it till you make it," pretending that they have a lot of experience when they do not.

"I think for a submissive, the best thing you can do is listen to your gut and don't be too desperate," Miss Kitty advises. "I know that's difficult, especially if you've been searching for this sort of dynamic. But instead of reaching out to people and saying like, 'Oh, can I be submissive' or 'can I call you Miss,' reach out to people not to be the submissive but to learn."

If someone is automatically trying to put you in a submissive role when you start chatting to them, they are not a proper Dom/me, Miss Kitty cautions. You are only their submissive if you are formally submitting to that individual Dom/me. "The same goes for people automatically calling me 'Miss'. I'm not your Miss. I have not consented to be your Miss. You can ask me questions or advice."

If you message a potential Dom/me to ask for advice and they immediately insist that you call them by a title, or they want to put you in a submissive place from the start, that is not a proper Dom/me, says Miss Kitty. Be particularly wary when these people get defensive if you ask questions.

"It is important to ask as many questions as you need

to give informed consent," Miss Kitty advises. "You can't give informed consent without all the information that you need to make that decision. So, if you're asking questions, and that dominant person is getting frustrated with you or telling you to just do as they say, that is a huge red flag and they are not real."

According to Miss Kitty, financial domination (or FinDom) is actually a small pocket of the real BDSM community. Online, however, it is a huge part of the community as there is a disproportionate number of subs to Dom/mes, leaving desperate submissives vulnerable to exploitation. Of course, there are professionals out there, but often, it is just opportunists milking you for easy money. If you want to make use of a professional service, make sure they are legit first, she advises.

———————◇———————

"Respect their boundaries and be mindful that you're taking on a lot of responsibility for somebody's physical and emotional safety as a Domme."
-Miss Kitty

———————◇———————

Advice for new Dommes

The most important piece of advice Miss Kitty has is to respect your submissives and their boundaries. Do not have set ideas on what your domination will look like from the get-go either. "Because, as you are exploring that with a submissive, those parameters can change depending on what the dynamics are at the time. Just because your submissive has said that they're happy for you to do X, Y and Z in that moment, that constant might have changed; it might be too much for them," she explains.

"Respect their boundaries and be mindful that you're taking on a lot of responsibility for somebody's physical and emotional safety as a Domme," Miss Kitty continues. "And if you're not willing to take on that responsibility in addition to the fun parts, maybe a sub-Domme dynamic isn't for you and you just like kinky sex, which is absolutely fine to explore consensually also. If you want a dynamic, you need to look after your sub."

Where possible, Miss Kitty herself will not inflict anything onto a sub that she has not experienced herself unless it's not physically possible due to her biological female anatomy. She will often try out toys, stress positions, different/new wax play, or electro-stimulation devices on herself first to better understand the sub's experience. This is done as a matter of research and assessment of risk rather than for her own sexual pleasure. "It's important to understand at which point it becomes unsafe," she says. "Now, I'm not saying that everybody's got to do it that way. But for me, I feel more comfortable pushing somebody to their limit, consensually, if I know what that limit feels like, or I've got a good enough idea."

Whatever you do, research is key. And if you cannot reach

out to a local community, actual literature is the next best thing, according to Miss Kitty. Not just blogs or advice from random strangers, but properly researched content. "It would be unsafe to enter into it without knowing the core of it," Miss Kitty concludes. "If you are not willing to do the work and wrap your head around how it works, then maybe BDSM is not for you."

Healing Through Gentle Femdom, Venus' Story

Venus could not relate to the Dommes she saw represented online. She was too soft, too kind—how could she ever dominate anyone? Meeting Luce showed her there was another way. A gentler way.

New to the Domme-life, US-based Venus (33) always thought she was too tame for femdom. That was until she met Luce (34). Through open and honest communication, Luce introduced Venus to a softer side of kink, a side he was very interested in.

Gentle femdom instantly appealed to Venus, who could not believe she had not encountered it online before. Together, the couple researched and explored, growing their dynamic from a foundation built on a strong emotional and sexual connection.

They found they had a lot of kinks in common, and both greatly enjoyed experimenting together as they crafted their unique dynamic.

Since then, this journey into the kinder side of kink has given Venus so much more than sexual satisfaction—which in itself is a great plus, of course. It has also helped with her confidence and learning to manage some of her anxieties.

Here follows Venus's story, a true story, shared in her own words during our audio interview. A story of self-discovery and healing; a story of amazing sex and a lot of fun; a story concluding with helpful advice for new subs and Dommes curious (or eager) to get into gentle femdom.

An Instant Connection

Venus considers herself a Switch these days—someone who enjoys both the Dom/me and sub roles. However, before meeting Luce, she was mainly sub-leaning. "This is my first time engaging in a relationship where I am in the dominant role, and it's fantastic. It's amazing!" says Venus.

The couple, who are both bisexual, met six months ago through a dating app, as one does these days. Although they both had profiles on more kinky apps (like FetLife), they actually found each other through OK Cupid—a popular dating app that boasts a large queer community.

Initially, there was no talk about a dynamic or kink, both partners simply liked each other and were both looking for a relationship.

They met for dinner only two days after they started chatting and their connection was "instantaneous." One of the deciding factors for Venus was how calm she felt during their first date and how easy it was to chat with Luce. "I didn't have the slightest bit of anxiety, and I'm anxious about everything," she remembers.

Thankfully the feeling was mutual, and they were instantly hooked on each other. From the very beginning, it was clear that they had a very strong sexual connection too. "I want him all the time. Constantly. I'm always staring at him. Because I think he's so sexy and beautiful."

They have been inseparable ever since.

Discovering Gentle Femdom

Thanks to their strong connection, the couple felt comfortable sharing their desires quite early on. It was Luce who initiated the conversation around gentle femdom.

Venus, who never had any partners interested in this role, had not thought about it much before. But after Luce explained to her what it actually entailed and why he was into it, she realized that gentle femdom really appealed to her.

Venus had never considered being a Domme. She did not feel like she fit the role. "I am not an aggressive person by any means. I can be a little sassy, but that's about as far as it goes. I tend to be extremely nurturing and just disgustingly sugary sweet when I'm in a relationship with someone. Prior to him bringing it up, I had not seen a lot of healthy or encouraging representation of gentle femdom."

A lot of what Venus had seen online was more on the aggressive side—not her style at all. That is why she never considered that femdom could be for her. After Luce raised his interest, she immediately started doing more research on the topic and getting more into it.

It took so much effort to find quality information online. A lot of the gentle femdom specifics Venus was curious about were not readily available online, and she had to dig to find the information.

Every Dynamic is Unique

Gentle femdom has changed Venus and Luce's relationship for the better. "It has completely opened up our dynamic in a really wonderful way because it just fits both of our personalities so well."

In their dynamic, they generally focus more on the sexual aspect of gentle femdom rather than living a 24/7 kinky life. To the outside world, they appear just like any other "vanilla" (non-kinky) couple with equal power dynamics.

Outside of the bedroom, Luce is opinionated and impulsive. When he wants something, he goes for it. But behind closed doors, it becomes 100% about what Venus wants. Luce derives pleasure from doing whatever Venus wants to do to him, she explains.

The couple likes to experiment and has found that they have a lot of kinks in common: nipple play, breastfeeding, pegging, and feminization to name a few. Also, activities involving "lots and lots of oil."

As Luce tends to be a bit more open and flexible, Venus has been the one to put boundaries and limits in place where she is personally uncomfortable. As she is not an aggressive person, she does not enjoy humiliation or heavy-impact play—she does not like to cause too much pain or leave any marks. So, that has been one of the boundaries she has put in.

But aside from that, whenever one of them wants to try out something new, they will always bring it up with the other partner and communicate their interest. They will ask if the other person would be willing to try this and how they feel about it, discussing it clearly before proceeding.

"So far, we have not yet come across something that we did not want to try together. So that's been a really, really fun experience."

Honest Communication Matters

Venus and Luce can talk about anything and everything—which has been great for Venus's anxiety. "It's been so natural from the start. I don't think I've ever been able to communicate with anyone the way I do with him."

She describes Luce as extremely communicative, honest,

and open about his feelings. This has been great for their relationship because Venus knows she can go to him with anything. This is important as the dynamic is led by her, and she wants to ensure Luce is comfortable and also enjoying their play.

They do not always know what they are doing. But they figure it out together through open communication and research. Neither party feels like they have to do something they don't want to do just to impress the other, or because they think that's what the other one wants.

"You have to make sure that both partners' needs are met and the only way to do that is by communicating what your needs are. This type of dynamic doesn't work unless you are able to really communicate."

They come to each other with all their wants, needs, or problems. "I feel so connected to him. Of course, through everything we do outside of the bedroom too, but a lot of it comes from our dynamic as you have to put a lot of trust in one another. It just doesn't work if you don't fully trust the other person. This really does help build that intimacy in such a fantastic way."

"Probably one of my favorite parts about our dynamic is that it is very, very flirty and we don't take things too seriously. We just want to have a good time together."
-Venus

Having Fun in the Bedroom

The couple keeps it light and fun in the bedroom. "Probably one of my favorite parts about our dynamic is that it is very, very flirty and we don't take things too seriously. We just want to have a good time together."

So, how *do* they come up with ideas of what to do in the bedroom? As Venus says, "not exactly the sexiest answer," but she does a lot of research. Learning about other couples and how their gentle femdom dynamic work has helped them craft their own foundation. Thanks to both of them being eager to put in the work and do the research, Venus feels that their dynamic has progressed a lot in a relatively short period of time.

And getting into the mood? That part is easy, according to Venus, because she finds her partner so sexy. They both have very high sex drives, so initiating is never a problem. She literally just gets him into a room and tells him it is happening—and he is very happy to oblige.

Learning to Domme

Stepping into the Domme-role did not come completely naturally at first. Venus says that each time they play, she has gotten stronger. When they first started out, she was overthinking things—always worrying about whether she was doing it right or whether Luce would like it.

The longer they have been together, the more confident Venus has become stepping into the Domme-role. Now she can easily tell Luce what she wants him to do, and she enjoys how it feels when they are engaging in that way. She has also learned more about what he likes, which has made her more confident in taking charge because she knows he wants it. "With ongoing practice, it just becomes easier, and it becomes more natural to slip into that state."

When Luce first asked Venus what she wanted sexually, she had no idea how to answer him. "It wasn't something I was used to being asked. It felt strange not to have an answer." As Luce's number one priority was to please and serve Venus, this answer was very important to him. As time went on and they explored more, it became easier for her to answer this question and prioritize her pleasure.

Venus says she simply did not know there was a name for the things she wanted. She had no framework for gentle femdom in particular. Now she does—which has improved her communication and built confidence in her Domme-role.

A Self-Healing Journey

Although Venus and Luce did not have any challenges with the sexual component of their dynamic, the challenge was a mental one for Venus. "I am a very anxious person and there were moments when my anxiety got the better of me." Luce helped her calm down and stop catastrophizing, to take a step back from the cliff edge. "His honesty helped me come back to reality."

The strong dynamic they have together has supported Venus in her healing journey, particularly in addressing some of her anxiety rooted in past traumas and experiences. "When we are together, I feel that connection so strongly and I trust him so thoroughly. It is helping me realize that a lot of these fears that I have are not based on anything. He's not doing anything that should make me feel that way; it's just my own brain making up reasons."

She initially viewed this as separate but realized it was just a different expression of their relationship—a powerful one at that. "When we are in the moment together, we are so connected and on the same level that it helps me remember—you know, we are two people who want to be together. We are two people who clearly work very well together and who love one another. And I just need to remember that whenever my brain wants to be wild and make up a bunch of 'what-ifs' that are not helpful."

As mentioned, gentle femdom has helped Venus with her confidence—not only inside the bedroom. Growing more confident as a Domme has allowed her to be more confident as a person.

Venus has made some big changes in her life over the past year, like going back to school and working out more to help her feel more confident in her body. This has allowed her to start feeling better about herself and her body, something she can express when in Domme mode. It all ties in together.

"Being a Domme to somebody else who loves our dynamic and loves who I am as a person, and loves what we do together, really helps me to see the value in myself and what I can offer other people." This has helped a lot with Venus's imposter syndrome feelings and second-guessing her self-worth.

Through femdom, Venus realized that she has a lot to offer people. "I am a strong and engaging person and I have someone here who wants to express that with me. So, it's just really made me feel very good. Just in myself and in my body. And in my relationship with my partner."

She didn't expect femdom to have this impact. The other steps she made very consciously, and this was something that just grew naturally from her discussions and experiences with Luce. But she's very happy that it did. "It's difficult to think of a dynamic that has been as fulfilling for me."

"You don't need to be hard, you don't need to be aggressive, you don't need to be super firm in order to be a dominant presence—you can exude that dominance in a very soft, gentle and caring way."
-Venus

Inaccurate Representation

Venus and Luce often talk about how difficult it is to find resources or porn that represent what they do. "I genuinely don't feel like a lot of the porn online is accurate at all." Although she found a few things here and there, it was "bonkers" to her that after months of searching, she only found a handful of things that she felt accurately represented their dynamic.

This is something that really bums her out, as she wished she had come across gentle femdom sooner in her life. Although she would have still needed a proper partner for it—and her current partner is the best one imaginable—Venus wishes she knew about this community earlier.

In particular, she wishes she knew that "you don't need to be hard, you don't need to be aggressive, you don't need to be super firm in order to be a dominant presence—you can exude that dominance in a very soft, gentle and caring way. And it's absolutely valuable and valid."

The lack of representation online forced Venus to view submission in very black-and-white, binary terms, which was very restrictive. "When you only see a certain representation of femdom for years and years, it can be difficult to realize that there are alternatives, and you don't have to engage in a type of relationship that doesn't suit you."

Venus describes herself as the type of person who cries

when she sees a beetle on its back, unable to get up—a real "gentle" Domme.

But because Venus thought Dommes had to fit the almost aggressive roles she saw online, she ended up in a lot of relationships where she was the sub—something she didn't find fully satisfying. "It was simply because I didn't have all the information and I didn't have the tools necessary to really be able to assess out where my place was on that spectrum."

But now she has truly found her place.

"I'm not the typical domineering person and that's just who I am. But I can be very sweet and still tell you what to do."

Look After Your Subs, Advice for Dommes

Venus's first word of advice to new gentle Dommes is to do your research about anything and everything. "If you are even mildly interested in something, do proper research to see how this can be safely and happily incorporated into your sex life." She suggests reading a lot and also speaking to others within the community to learn from real-life experiences.

When it comes to engaging with your sub, Venus encourages open discussions to ensure you have valid consent and they are comfortable with what is happening. "Don't push anything on them because that's not cool. Subs are people too. They are people made to worship you, but they're still people."

Although her pleasure comes first, it is important for Venus to make sure Luce is also pleasured and happy too. "I want to do things he's going to enjoy. That's why understanding yourself and your own sexuality, as well as understanding your partner's is critical in crafting a healthy, happy and sexy dynamic."

She gets joy from giving Luce care and "treating him like the good boy that he is." Boys also deserve flowers or maybe a cup of coffee if you wake up first. "Just because they're your sub, it doesn't mean that you can't do nice things for them. It just makes them more motivated to do nice things for you later."

———————◇———————

"...people should focus on what type of relationship you want first before just trying to jump into the sex part."
-Venus

———————◇———————

Do Not Call Me Mistress—Advice for Subs

Venus explains that she would find it very off-putting if a stranger or someone she barely knew addressed her by a title like Miss or Mistress. "It's weird."

"I think that people should focus on what type of relationship you want first before just trying to jump into the sex part." If you want a romantic relationship with this dynamic and not just pure sex, then you have to work on the romance first—just like with any vanilla relationship.

"I am not just here to provide a service for you. If you're paying me for it, then it's different. But if that's not what we're doing, then don't use me. I am a person with my own wants, needs, desires, and opinions. Do not see me as just a vehicle for your own pleasure."

When chatting to people online or just in general—"be an actual person." Don't just try and force people into the role of Domme or sub. "Until you're actually in a dynamic, you can't just call someone Mistress—it's rude and disrespectful. I would be very uncomfortable if someone referred to me in that way. I am not your Domme, so please don't."

She also advises subs to do their research to find out what they are into and what they want. "The more that you understand yourself, the better that you will be able to bring this up to your partner in an open-minded way, so you can have a discussion about it and see if it's something that you two can do together."

"Just because you are a sub doesn't mean that you can't be involved in some of the decision-making processes of what you do in the dynamic. So, take a little bit of agency in that way and just say, 'hey, I like this, is that something that we can incorporate?' And then your Domme can discuss that with you and hopefully, you can come to an agreement that works for you both."

Subs are also encouraged to recognize their power. No matter what happens in a scene, the sub has the power to stop it with their safe word(s). This gives subs the majority of power in scenes because their comfort is what's driving everything.

Subs who are looking for Dommes should also remember that not every Domme is actually going to be appropriate for you, explains Venus. You do not know how they like to express their dominance or whether it is compatible with your submissiveness. "Don't just go in assuming that any Domme is going to be just perfect for you. Because that's not how it works. There needs to be compatibility."

Another big piece of advice to subs is to not just go for sex—there is so much more to gentle femdom. "I feel like if my partner and I did not have that emotional intimacy, the sexual part of it would not be even half as fulfilling as it is. It's because we trust each other that it is such a good experience for both of us."

MADAM MAYHEM FINDS HER SEXUAL FREEDOM

"For me, submission is more about their pleasure. I am here to take care of them." -Madam Mayhem (41), Mommy-Domme/ Pleasure-Domme/ Service-Domme

Madam Mayhem is an Australian-born pansexual switch who now lives in the UK. She runs a gentle femdom OnlyFans account, and also enjoys being a kinkster in her personal dating life.

This is Mayhem's story of reconnecting with her sexuality after a repressive marriage. Of how she worked on herself and her mental health, grew as a person, and learned to prioritize her sexual needs. There is more to a kinky life than meets the eye.

Getting into Kink

Madam Mayhem ventured into kink about three years ago after her five-year marriage ended. Her kink journey was born from what was lacking in her marriage: "He was a wonderful human, and I'm still in touch with him, but there was definitely a disparity in terms of our sex drive and our sexuality."

Unbeknownst to her, Mayhem's ex-husband was still holding on to traumas from his past. This affected how he interacted with her—both in and out of the bedroom. "I inadvertently felt shamed for being a sexual person and suggesting new things or initiating sex."

As such, Mayhem had to suppress a part of herself during the five years of their marriage. "So when the marriage ended, I finally felt free and ready to explore. I wanted to have the antithesis of what happened in my marriage and reconnect with my sexuality, find out what I really enjoy. And mostly just get out there and have some fun."

Enter Madam Mayhem

After a separation, Mayhem started dating again in May 2020. Initially, her experiences were fairly vanilla (non-kinky). She was gradually rediscovering her sexual self and started buying more lingerie and sex toys.

She slowly ventured into kinkier dating sites like Feeld. Naturally, the conversations became gradually kinkier too.

Mayhem started chatting to a 21-year-old guy who loved the idea that she was a "cougar." They had a lot of similar kinks and he was the one who initially encouraged her to start an OnlyFans account.

As a natural exhibitionist, this idea appealed to Mayhem. She decided it was worth exploring. Despite initial concern about word getting out at her vanilla job, she did it anyway.

"I was terrified for the first month. I was freaking out, threatening to take it down every day. But then I started getting subscribers and people were very complimentary about what I was posting. That built up my confidence."

Mayhem built her social media presence around this and created a blog to write about her experiences. She is also an affiliate for various sex toy companies. "All of it funds my lingerie habit."

Mayhem only responds to DMs from registered OnlyFans subscribers, but they're not always sexual. Some just want advice. "Many guys sign up simply for a safe space to talk about their kinks and explore their submissive side."

She also offers custom femdom videos and Mistress sexting sessions, but that is as far as she goes in the commercial realm. She admits she receives daily requests for pegging services but safety concerns have prevented her from exploring this in-person activity.

Dating Kinky

These days, Madam Mayhem prefers to date younger

partners and gladly leans into the age gap. While pansexual, she finds herself predominantly attracted to men. "Women are difficult to flirt with," she jokes.

The number one theme among the younger men she has dated is a need to explore their submissive side, but not feeling comfortable (or able) to do so with women their own age. "There is a lot of societal pressure to fit into those gender norms and be masculine and dominant." Mayhem's age helped break down this barrier, allowing the men to open up about the desires they want to explore or express.

A Traditional Upbringing

Mayhem grew up in Australia and describes her upbringing as "heteronormative." She was attracted to women from her early 20s but did not really think about it much at the time. Her upbringing and the societal norms back home prevented her from exploring this side.

"I come from a family of avoidant types," she says, "I had to leave Australia. It was just too smothering for me back there." Her family is still there, but Mayhem finds it hard to share this side of her with them. Most have no idea about her kinky life. Mayhem told one of her sisters, but the conversation didn't get far. Her sister did not ask a single question.

This restrictive upbringing also played a part in making Madam Mayhem who she is today. As the oldest child, Mayhem had to put in a lot of work in therapy to process her feelings of responsibility towards her younger siblings.

Growing up, she was constantly told to set an example and take care of her sisters. "That's where a lot of my nurturing side comes from. Through femdom, I have found an interesting way to express this side of me."

———————◇———————

"It's more about taking care of that person and giving them that release, that pleasure, helping them fulfill that."
-Madam Mayhem

———————◇———————

Mental Health Matters

In the aftermath of the marriage, Mayhem started seeing a therapist. This health journey has run alongside her kink journey. "It's been interesting to see how that's impacted and helped me recover from what damage was done in the marriage and how it's helping me explore."

Mental health is very important to Madam Mayhem. "Being on the receiving end of some pretty bad dominant behavior and having had some traumatic experiences myself, when I am in the Dominant role, I am so hugely aware of the other person's mental state."

That is why aftercare negotiation is important for

her—making sure the submissive feels safe. "They are trusting me, and I would never want to breach that trust because being submissive is such a vulnerable state." She wants to provide a safe space for them to indulge their submissive tendencies, to allow them the freedom of such a release. "But I would never do that for someone unless I could always put their mental health first."

Mayhem considers herself a Switch and has personally experienced the dark side of fake Doms online: guys who have no idea what being a Dom is all about. These fake Doms generally do not listen and have no regard for consent. That's *not* what Mayhem wants for the submissives she engages with.

An age gap also adds responsibility. Mayhem places herself in the caregiver role and often considers herself a bit of a Mommy-Domme. She has tried all aspects of femdom but finds the maternal approach feels most natural to her. She previously engaged a submissive who was into pain and humiliation. After a couple of sessions, she realized that the harsh treatment was not something she enjoyed: "It's just not me."

"For me, submission is more about their pleasure. I am here to take care of them, to give them pleasure." That's why she likes labels like Mommy-Domme, Pleasure-Domme, or Service-Domme. "I feel like that's my jam. It's more about taking care of that person and giving them that release, that pleasure, helping them fulfill that."

But Mayhem is no mother. She draws a clear distinction between taking on a nurturing role in the bedroom and taking care of someone full-time. "I want someone who is submissive in the bedroom but not in life. I chose not to have children. I'm not having one in a relationship. These are very different areas. I will not be your mother in life too."

Raising her Standards

"Kink is very much my life—not just for online." Mayhem cannot see herself ever being in a sexually vanilla relationship again. She now exclusively dates other kinksters. "I cannot imagine having to box that part of myself back up again for someone else."

Thanks to therapy and introspection, Mayhem's self-respect has grown and she no longer settles for anything less than what she deserves. She has a better understanding of herself and her own needs and will not compromise. This has inadvertently led to a slow-down in her dating life because she won't "put up with any shit."

Mayhem had a partner last year, but experimentation with non-monogamy complicated things. The problem was not the non-monogamy per se, but rather her partner going against the agreements they had made. "I was absolutely gutted. It was my first experience of non-monogamy with somebody I loved. I'm trying to work through that because I don't want it to ruin the possibility of non-monogamy for me."

In the aftermath of the breakup, Mayhem has not dated very much. Instead, she has focused her attention on healing and raising her standards. "Before I wasn't even getting my bare minimum needs met and I would settle for so much less. Now I don't want it unless it's good for me."

She still goes on dates from time to time but nothing serious has grown from that at this stage. "I would love to be in a relationship and have a kink dynamic. But you can't force these things."

Curse of the Switch

"I feel like being a Switch is a blessing and a curse," says Mayhem. While playing both roles technically provides her with some variety, she rarely gets to indulge her own submissive side. In three years, only two men have successfully dominated her.

For the most part, Mayhem finds herself in the dominant role because she prefers younger people. She's dated plenty of Switches but always finds herself dominating because female Dommes are harder to come by—"And once you settle into a dynamic, you actually can't shift roles that easily."

"You have to arm yourself with knowledge or risk getting into precarious situations that could potentially hurt you."
-Madam Mayhem

Dear Submissive, A Word of Advice

Mayhem is a firm believer in research, and not "just throwing yourself into the kinky world uninformed." Do not just go out looking for a dominant partner immediately. Familiarize yourself with the ideas of aftercare and consent. Learn about Risk-Aware/ Accepted Consensual Kink (RACK) and other good practices so that you can spot the fakes.

The lack of education about consent and other key kink topics frustrates her. "People go out there thinking they can just make it up as they go along. It doesn't work that way. You have to arm yourself with knowledge or risk getting into precarious situations that could potentially hurt you."

Unfortunately, the submissive young men she engages with often are not very patient. They don't want to do the research first. "They're just like: well, I want this and I want to do it now. They don't really think through the consequences."

When a new sub tells her they want to be pegged, Mayhem asks if they have ever been rimmed, or at least used a toy on themselves (like a butt plug). If not, she advises them to explore that first to test the waters—find out if it is the feeling they enjoy and not just the idea. By exploring on their own first, a sub will know more about their own pleasure and limits by the time they play with a partner.

The taboo around anything anal for cis-gendered heterosexual men is a big challenge, according to Mayhem. Many of these men think that if they can find a woman to peg them, the act of enjoying anal pleasure will not be frowned upon as much by society. This misguided, desperate approach can lead to potentially risky encounters with fake Dommes. "There is a bit of common sense involved that most men don't think about. They just think about the end goal and what they want, forgetting to educate themselves and to be patient until they find the right person."

Mayhem cautions against trying to force a connection: "If the chemistry isn't there, you can't fake it." She's been on numerous dates where there's simply been no chemistry, but the sub tries to force it out of desperation. "Not every Domme is going to suit you."

Aftercare is Not Optional

Mayhem reminds subs (and Dommes) to be mindful of the often-overlooked Domme-drop. Subs are not the only ones who potentially have to deal with intense emotions after a scene. That is why aftercare is important for all partners involved.

Mayhem recounts dating a male sub who was into pain play and humiliation. After the session, he collected his belongings and walked away with no aftercare whatsoever. "I had massive Domme-drop after a session with him, and that really caught me off guard. I had no idea that this was possible and I was pretty messed up afterward."

This was a big learning curve for Mayhem. "Unfortunately, I find that male subs sometimes just want to use a Domme to meet their needs. But they forget that it's a two-way street. Even if they say that they are there to serve you and for your pleasure, it can still inherently be quite selfish—they are only doing what they're doing to get themselves off. They forget about participating in aftercare."

Approaching a Domme

It might seem obvious, but not all Dommes are the same. They want different things and have different boundaries. Some practice femdom in their personal life only, while others focus on paid services. Madam Mayhem falls somewhere in between these categories. She enjoys femdom and kinky play in her personal life but also accepts payments for certain services.

She states clearly on all her profiles that she does not accept unsolicited DMs, and only replies to her OnlyFans subscribers. But Mayhem still gets bombarded with messages from people insisting on responses, often disrespectfully.

"Guys slide into my DMs all the time, calling me Mommy off the bat. You are not my submissive. We have not negotiated honorifics. Why are you calling me Mommy? The audacity to just think about what *they* want. They do not recognize that there is a human being on the other side of that chat and that you have to treat them with respect. Not just immediately assume they're going to do your bidding."

It boils down to being a decent human being, being respectful, and adhering to social norms when reaching out to a complete stranger. "Just don't be creepy. Don't be rude. That person doesn't owe you anything—especially not their valuable time and energy."

Advice for Dommes

Mayhem stresses that a Domme does not have to stick to one particular type of dominance. "Kink is what you make it out to be and you can customize it to suit you."

It is about figuring out what you enjoy. How do *you* want to be dominant? Mayhem suggests you do not force yourself to be a certain kind of way based on the representation you see—either online or in real life. "That's how I started out and it made me feel very inadequate. I felt like I couldn't call myself a Domme because I wasn't the typical Mistress-type."

This made Mayhem reluctant to go to kink clubs because she was worried they would look down on her as inferior. "It was hard to get my head around the fact that I don't have to fit into that stereotype. Figure out what femdom looks like for you."

Just like for subs, she recommends that Dommes do as

much research as they can to improve their knowledge of femdom. She learned a lot from following online accounts of reputable and well-established kinksters. "There is a community, you are not alone. Kinksters are generally very open-minded and non-judgmental. They genuinely want to help you on your journey. If you can, dive into your community."

"Kink is what you make it out to be and you can customize it to suit you."
-Madam Mayhem

Playing Safe

Sadly, Madam Mayhem does not get too involved in any physical community anymore. She is introverted and simply does not feel safe going to sex clubs as a single female—there have been too many instances of women being assaulted after leaving the clubs.

"I basically need a male chaperone with me or I can't go. I don't feel safe. It's actually difficult to get into the community because of this."

Mayhem says she would prefer to wait until she has a

partner to go with her to sex clubs so that she can feel safe and enjoy it, rather than force the situation and have to worry about safety.

Find Your People

Mayhem is selective about whom she tells about her kinky life. Luckily, she has a great group of friends who are fully accepting of her journey of sexual discovery. "It might not be for them, but they've been so supportive. They can see the impact it's had on my life and how healing and confidence-building it's been for me."

She has met other friends through her kinky experiences. "You know, guys that I dated and maybe the chemistry wasn't there, or things just petered out for whatever reason. I now have a beautiful group of friends who know everything about me. And I don't have to hide anything, which is really lovely."

Mayhem says her candidness with the topic has even inspired some of her coupled friends to experiment with their sex lives. Many have thanked her for sharing her experiences and opening them up to the possibilities.

It's a Journey

Madam Mayhem's most important piece of advice can be summed up in a single word—patience. "Accept that kink is a lifetime journey. The more you get involved, the more you discover. The more you discover, the more you find new things you want to try. You need to be patient and trust that things will happen at the right time."

SUB TO DOMME: GODDESS PINKY FINDS JOY IN HER 40S

Despite typically identifying as submissive, Goddess Pinky recently took a sub of her own, uncovering her inner gentle Domme in the process—"Who knew it could be so much fun?"

Many know US-based Goddess Pinky (41) by her stage name, Ivana Coquêtú. A creative burlesque performer widely known in the online BDSM community, Goddess Pinky has always been very vocal about consent and risk-aware kink. Before the great Tumblr sexual content purge of 2018, her page had attracted more than 40,000 followers.

Her Tumblr page provided insight into her life as a long-distance submissive, sharing advice for others in the community. At the time, the 'Daddy-Dom' to her 'Princess' lived in another city. After more than three years of living apart, they finally eloped and began a 24/7 dynamic. That was eight years ago, and they now have a two-year-old together.

She had always been submissive in the bedroom unless it was to take on a role as a service top—or if she was training new subs for her husband. In all these prior experiences, she had found being the dominant partner to be "de-energizing" and thus dismissed it as "not for me."

Since then, a lot has happened in Goddess Pinky's life...

Changing Times

The past year has seen a lot of change for Goddess Pinky. For one thing, she began exploring burlesque, an experience she describes as "really liberating." Sadly, she has also experienced a lot of adversity over the past 12 months—first when her mother passed away, and then when the relationship with her husband developed a tear.

It was during this period that her future *pet* (a type of submissive) re-entered Pinky's life and they started experimenting with her in a dominant role.

Pinky and her pet (33) have known each other for around eight years, but only started playing together in a kinky way in 2022. He is not her primary relationship, but he gets along well with her husband and their respective partners. The whole family—kids included—often enjoy activities and outings together.

Pinky and her pet do not consider themselves very romantic and their dynamic is not particularly verbally sentimental. Yet there are clearly feelings involved. "We have a very deep connection and I think about him a lot," Pinky explains.

She says it is the little things he does that warm her heart the most, like how he wins her stuffed toys from the claw machine and helps around the house.

Sex is a Weapon

Before marrying her Daddy-Dom, Pinky was married to a very conservative partner. Their relationship was full of kink-shaming and she felt like she could not quite be herself. But today, at 41, she feels freer and more herself than she ever has before.

Pinky is all about rewriting the narrative around what your 40s are like for women. "This is the hottest, sexiest, and most control of my life I've ever been in, and I would never go back." She describes fitting into a normal patriarchal society as "hard" and enjoys her newfound freedom.

"I'm about defying feminist standards and smashing the patriarchy. Sex is a weapon in some ways and I'm taking it back."

Gaining a Pet

Because her previous marriage was so conservative, Pinky

had never attended any kink events. This all changed when she married her Daddy-Dom and they moved to Savannah, Georgia together.

Being new to the city, Pinky had no friends or family around. Her husband worked a lot and had a crazy schedule, leaving him unavailable much of the time.

Still, eager to join their local kink community, the couple planned to attend a munch (a kinky event for like-minded people to meet). Unfortunately, work prevented Pinky's husband from attending with her.

So, dressed in a cute little sailor dress, Pinky headed off to her first kink munch—alone. "I had no idea I was attractive at that point. I learned that through kink."

At the munch, Pinky befriended some people sitting across from her, including her future-submissive pet. He did not speak much though, especially not to Pinky. She was convinced he did not like her. Even at subsequent meetings, he was virtually mute around her despite chatting to her husband like an old friend. Turns out he was in fact obsessed with her but did not want to offend her husband.

While part of the Savannah Underground scene, Pinky and her future-pet would sometimes play together as subs, putting on a scene for others at the party. But they never interacted much outside of that.

During this time, Pinky's pet played with a lot of strangers where aftercare was limited at best. She grew concerned about this, about him, and one day asked a friend for his phone number so she could check in on him.

Pinky remembers a time when she covered him in a blanket after a scene, even putting lotion on him after someone else whipped him. She once gave him some chocolate too. Yet he hardly spoke to her.

That is how it stayed for years. Eventually, both Pinky and her pet moved to different cities—he to New York and she to Atlanta. 2020 brought with it a global pandemic, and Pinky lost touch with her former Savannah kink friends.

Then in 2021, she got a message from him. Her had moved back to Atlanta and wanted to meet up...

It's the Little Things

Pinky was eager to catch up with a friend from her Savannah Underground past and invited her pet-to-be over. They were all supposed to hang out together, but as usual, her husband had work commitments and was unable to join.

Nothing sexual happened on that day, nothing kinky. They just chatted and caught up. But then her pet did something that has stuck with Pinky to this day—the reason she called him back. He asked her if he could take out her trash. "That was weird. And cute."

Pinky messaged him to ask why he did that. "*I mean, I appreciate it. Thank you. I don't want to sound ungrateful but that's not a normal thing people offer when they leave your home, right?"* He confessed to being a service sub and enjoying chores like that, plus impact play.

Her pet-to-be mustered up all his courage and told Pinky that he would enjoy playing together if she was interested, but that he would also be perfectly fine with doing vanilla (non-kinky) stuff together and just being friends. He offered to help with the dishes and walking the dogs, *"whatever you need, feel free to ask."*

"What about foot massages?" Pinky asked.

"Yes, absolutely foot massages," he replied.

She added: *"What about foot massages* and *eating pussy?"*

"Absolutely!" He was keen.

"Well, I don't know about option two but I won't take it off the table completely," she replied.

It was settled, he started coming over on Thursdays—Pinky's day for other partners.

In addition to her husband, Pinky had another dominant partner at the time who visited her on Thursday nights. So Pinky scheduled time with her pet during the day on Thursdays. They would walk the dogs, he'd do the dishes, and engage in some impact play—putting Pinky's impressive sex toy collection to good use.

Pinky had to remind him that she was primarily a sub—she was not used to dishing out the spankings.

———————◇———————

"At one point, I was crying I was laughing so hard. I didn't know that this was supposed to be this much fun."
-Goddess Pinky

———————◇———————

So Much Fun

Pinky's pet accepted that she was not dominant by nature, but he was willing to explore.

During their first play session, after discussing limits and consent, Pinky got out her old-school yardstick and "beat the living shit out of this man." Yet, they were having so much fun and laughing harder than she had ever laughed in her life, she remembers.

Pinky even pulled out her electric zapper, sending both of them into hysterical laughing fits. "At one point, I was crying I was laughing so hard. I didn't know that this was supposed to be this much fun." She still considers that day as one of the top five most fun moments of her entire life.

But even when she beat him so hard that her hand went blue, her pet did not use his safe word. Pinky was concerned she was going too far, so she put down the yardstick, dumped a glass of ice water over him, and had him massage her feet.

They had not developed that part of their relationship yet, so the aftercare was initially slightly awkward. But it was important for Pinky to administer it anyway. "You just beat the shit out of someone—if you're not willing to provide aftercare, you shouldn't get in this scenario."

Her pet helped her clean the house afterward and she gave him a little bit of chocolate to perk up his dopamine levels.

Do It Again

After the yardstick day, Pinky and her pet agreed that they had fun and wanted to do it again. So they kept playing. They introduced more elements like chastity play, orgasm denial, some humiliation, and teasing. They developed a great friendship and mutual respect.

Pinky would shove her feet in his mouth from time to time, but their relationship was not particularly sexual at all. It was just kinky play. Often they just did vanilla things like chores and listening to music.

Then, one weekend, that changed.

They had all gone away together for a trip—Pinky, her husband, her dominant partner, her pet, and her husband's former partner. Pinky's dominant partner instructed her to go down on her pet and she happily obliged. She also pegged her pet for the first time during this trip—something he had always wanted.

Pinky had pegged both men and women before but had never enjoyed the experience. "It was de-energizing, clumsy and awkward." This time it felt different—not weird at all. "This was fucking fun. Everything with him is fun."

After the trip, her pet stayed an extra night to help clean up and enjoy extra time with her. That's where their relationship really started to take off.

Pinky eventually found herself aroused by play sessions with her pet. At first, she did not touch him sexually—he would always wear a chastity cage. She would just get him really aroused and send him home, denying him pleasure and leaving him humiliated. Then she would do things with her dominant partner or husband.

A Break-Up

After their group trip, things became more complicated for Pinky and her dominant partner. He started giving off mixed signals.

They enjoyed an amazing foursome together on their trip, but a few days after, he shamed Pinky for being polyamorous and raising children in what he deemed an "unhealthy setting." He wanted to pursue a monogamous relationship with someone else and was not willing to tell his new partner about Pinky because he was afraid it would ruin his chances.

It's important for Pinky that her partners are involved in her day-to-day life. "I'm a very busy person and if you can't come over and plug into my daily life, then it's not going to work for me. If you can't act normal and have a sandwich with my kids and be our friend, then we don't need to be doing this. I'm not in this to be secretive. If we have an intimate relationship, you need to be able to be around my family, because I'm tired of keeping secrets."

This was a deal-breaker for Pinky. Their relationship ended immediately. She would not tolerate being shamed, so she kicked him out.

Little did she know that this ending was about to trigger a whole new beginning with her submissive partner...

Getting Sexual

On the Thursday that things ended with her dominant partner, Pinky's pet was already scheduled to visit. She warned him of her emotional state but he insisted on coming over anyway.

In an attempt to cheer her up, her pet sent a picture of the six stuffed animals he won at the arcade. Pinky's inner child is easily soothed with stuffed animals ("they're my favorite thing in the world"), so it did in fact help. She took the coincidence as cosmic timing.

That's when their relationship started to shift.

Then, in November 2022, her pet started eating her out. Two months later, they started having sex—lots of sex. They had many conversations about this before and acknowledged the potential emotional complications, but they were both willing to explore further.

Pinky has since found her Mommy-Domme side really emerging, increasingly enjoying things like making her pet ask for permission. Together, they have created a safe space where they enjoy spending time together in many different ways. Sometimes they sit in silence for almost an hour, just sensually touching.

Having the space to freely ask for things has become very important to Pinky. "It's been incredibly healing to have a space where I don't feel like a bitch for asking someone to do stuff. I'm not nagging, the submissive is actually thriving off it. It's given me permission to not feel shitty about being a strong woman."

Meanwhile, she has created a safe space for her pet to be more feminine and explore his sexuality. "We often talk about all the boxes we tick for each other, boxes we didn't even know we needed."

Risk-Aware Kink

Boundaries and safety are very important to Pinky. The Savannah Underground community put great emphasis on teaching consent and risk-aware kink, using the stoplight system at their parties (*red for stop, yellow to slow down/ reevaluate, and green for "all good"*). As both Pinky and her pet came from this community, they already spoke the same language of consent, making it easier to engage in play.

People new to the kink scene often miss this. Pinky reiterates that you need to ensure a clear understanding of safe words and boundaries upfront. While it is the dominant's responsibility to raise this, the submissive person has to have the emotional capacity to speak about their own limits and to stand firm in them. "Or else you shouldn't play with them."

"You don't want to really hurt someone. And if you do, that's not consensual kink. No one's signing up for unbearable mental trauma. This should be a space for healing, not for making new wounds. Too often I see it as a space for abuse. And that's not why I'm here."

As a gentler Domme who proclaims that she does it "in the name of love," Pinky is happy to physically hurt someone if they want her to. But she needs to know that they understand how safe words work and that they are on the same page.

———◇———

"You don't want to really hurt someone. And if you do, that's not consensual kink. This should be a space for healing, not for making new wounds."
-Goddess Pinky

———◇———

Speak Your Words

Pinky finds that submissives, especially men, will often claim to be fine after a scene despite feeling the opposite. "I don't know if male submissives always have the emotional language, or awareness, to say, 'Hey, I'm feeling down right now'." Society dictates that men must not show weakness, which can make it even harder for them to identify and express their feelings.

Pinky feels bad for the plight of men in this regard. "I can't imagine trying to learn what my emotions mean in adulthood only. Women are told to choke down their feelings and hide them in a room. But at least we're taught to understand them. Men are often literally physically abused for showing emotion as boys. And it really fucks them up."

Pinky uses a lot of this feminist, anti-patriarchal language, which can be confusing for the men in her life. They often perceive her as a man-hater. This is not the case at all though.

"I love men, but y'all need some help. We've got to learn to drop the defensiveness over masculinity and realize it's not about hating men. It's about trying to fix the problem. And it's not you—you're not the problem. It's the systems that we all subscribe to that have caused the problem."

Check-in with Your Partner

Pinky encourages submissives to highlight non-negotiable requirements to their dominant partners. Personally, she requires her partners to check in with her within two days of a play session. "If you're going to choke me, slap me, degrade me (consensually) you have a responsibility to check on me in the next 24 to 48 hours. It doesn't mean that we're going to run away and have children together. But you should care about my well-being because I let you do those things to me."

Pinky offers presentations on consent and also shares these with anyone interested in playing with her. If that scares them off, then goodbye. She doesn't want people like that in her life. "You don't like my stoplight consent system? What I'm hearing is that you don't respect boundaries. I'm not trying to get assaulted because of your misunderstanding of what I said."

Safe spaces are very important to Pinky. "Kink is supposed to be a safe space to explore things that you cannot explore in any other realm. I can't fathom another way. Even if it's a paid exchange for sex work, you should leave feeling like you received what you came for, not feeling traumatized by the experience."

Aftercare is Essential

Experience in the submissive role means Pinky understands the connection a sub has with their dominant partner; how important aftercare and being valued is—"Without aftercare or gratitude, it can lead to a lot of drama."

When she had previously tried to play as a dominant, she found herself being too nice. "I can be really mean—consensually. But I feel like shit about it unless there's a way to reset the balance afterward (which differs from person to person)." This is where aftercare comes in and having honest, open, and vulnerable conversations. But it can be uncomfortable to get to that point with someone.

That is why Pinky is not willing to engage in kinky play with someone without a way to restore balance before transitioning back into the real world. "It fucks up your head; it really does fuck with your emotion."

"The real life of living this way is not the fantasy that we have online. It's much more complicated. There are a lot of emotional things that surface and really vulnerable conversations that have to take place in order to have a healthy relationship when you like to be consensually physically abused."

She wants to use kink to create healing experiences rather than traumatic ones. "Too often dominance and submission are painted as trauma-creating spaces, but for most of us it's a way to reclaim something." She and her pet have created a healing space—one that Pinky didn't even know she needed.

———————◇———————

"As a dominant, you have to keep your submissive safe. Whether or not their needs seem silly to you, they're not silly."
-Goddess Pinky

———————◇———————

Advice for Dommes

While the talk of boundaries and consent might not seem sexy on paper, it is very important. A formal contract is not always necessary, but Pinky encourages some form of agreement between a Dom/me and their sub.

It is important that partners give informed consent. If not capable of doing so, Pinky advises that dominant partners start slowly, especially with inexperienced subs who do not yet know their limits. "You don't want to unintentionally assault someone. You do not want to live with that."

Due diligence is key to avoiding hurting yourself or someone else. "There is a lot of abuse in this lifestyle and abuse is never okay. And if you're falling into the abuse cycle because you're in this lifestyle, you need to stop and reevaluate and renegotiate boundaries. Because that does happen."

Kinky dynamics can be emotionally confusing, which is why it's so important to have a support system. "You need to be around people who also are in the lifestyle, which can be hard to find. Sadly, a lot of people are just out there to prey upon others. Luckily, there are many resources out there to protect us. Find them. You have to keep yourself safe." That's why things like the stoplight system and the proper vetting partners are so important.

"As a dominant, you have to keep your submissive safe. Whether or not their needs seem silly to you, they're not silly. It's not your space to determine what their needs are for emotional health, and for physical safety."

Everyone has their own story with different traumas. You never know what will trigger someone. If a sub goes into a fight-or-flight response, they are no longer able to play and make decisions. A dominant partner needs to be able to recognize that and stop—"Anything further is abuse."

"Build Trust, Then Tie"

Pinky cautions against chasing the erotic scenes you see online. Most of these scenes are staged, simply offering a highlight of a real engagement. There is so much more that goes on behind the scenes to ensure everyone's safety—physically and emotionally. "We have a responsibility to leave each other either the same or better than we found them. Otherwise, you're doing damage and no one wants that done to them."

Things like breath play and waterboarding can be very dangerous even when you know what you're doing. Pinky's advice is to start slow—do not immediately attempt the most extreme level. Even with things like tying someone up—a very common fetish—do not tie their hands at first. "Build trust, then tie more."

Pinky explains that when you are physically smaller or weaker than the person you're playing with and throw in an element of restraint, your brain can be fooled into thinking you are the prey. That is why Pinky is so worried about coercion, especially when the dominant partner pushes too far. It is easy for a sub to agree to something that breaks their boundaries while in such a vulnerable state. Submissives cannot offer clear consent while in this state.

"If you're twice my size, you have to understand that it's not safe for me to say no, and my brain knows that—consciously or unconsciously. So, my brain tells me to just go along with it, even if it's something I didn't intend to do." That's why it's so important to have a safe space to talk about a scene afterward (and prior).

"Society has taught us that wearing our boundaries down is sexy and it is not."

The fact that this lifestyle is so taboo makes it very hard for the right people to meet up because everyone's trying to hide it. They do not know what to ask for—especially men living in more repressed societies. "Often it makes people act crazy and causes a lot more assault and shame than it should." That's why Pinky cares so much about progressing the language within the community.

————————◇————————

"I don't believe shame has a place in sex."
-Goddess Pinky

————————◇————————

No More Shame

Pinky runs a sex-positive household and always answers questions around this topic truthfully—even from her 12-year-old stepdaughter. "I feel like in the absence of information, we can create really, really fucked up stories in our head." She wants to break the cycle of emotional damage parents cause when teaching their children sex is shameful.

"I don't believe shame has a place in sex. I don't believe that there's shame in our bodies, or shame in wanting to have sex. I believe that there is shame in misusing people as objects. I don't mean objectifying when it's consensual. I mean consuming people and possessing them." Pinky believes sex should be love and healing.

Shame is one of the key factors that put Pinky off organized religion—where sex is often bashed as shameful. This does not stop her from being close to her God. Pinky believes that just because you are kinky does not mean you cannot have a good relationship with your God. In fact, kink makes her feel *closer* to her God. "The desire was put inside you to connect in that way, so let's just heal this religious trauma."

MISS LIYA: A NATURAL DOMINANCE

A Domme in both her personal and professional life, Miss Liya sees kink as a way to help people find their own identity and heal through personal growth.

Miss Liya (21) is from the Midwest in the US and has never felt the need to be submissive. "I never realized just how different my needs were from the women generally portrayed in the media."

At first, she did not know that the way she approached her sexual encounters was actually considered BDSM. She always enjoyed obedience and a rewards system in her personal relationships but did not realize that this was in fact kink. "I thought it was just how I loved people."

Liya really enjoys helping people with discussions on trauma and personal growth—she always has. "Only later did I realize how much those feelings of vulnerability are tied into kink and power-play."

Practicing Kink

Liya has a boyfriend who is her full-time submissive. Additionally, she also offers pro-Domme services—online exclusively. She currently has a full-time submissive online, plus others who come and go. Having boundaries and clearly communicating them to all her submissives is very important to her.

"My relationships are built on mutual trust and a mutual benefit understanding." When someone expresses interest in pursuing what she offers, Liya usually begins by making sure they understand what she expects of them. She also gets a better feel for what they need to feel more comfortable with themselves.

In her professional relationships, she usually offers a guiding hand, helping them find their own identity through fashion, discussing their past relationships and needs, and talking about what they want when it comes to their core values.

As part of her professional services, subs often pay tribute for Miss Liya's attention. "I tell them early on that I expect tributes and spoiling." If submissives online want her attention or feel grateful for her time and energy, they will send her money, buy her clothes, or send food deliveries, for example.

"It's just so important to have that communication upfront and to be so clear about what I have to offer and where we stand. Otherwise it just complicates things further down the line."

———————◇———————

"I believe that gentle femdom approaches kink as a means to make the other feel nurtured and cared for."
-Miss Liya

———————◇———————

Kinky and Kind

Liya considers herself a gentle Domme. "I believe that gentle femdom approaches kink as a means to make the other feel nurtured and cared for. I think there's still a very clear dynamic between the dominant and the submissive, but the submissive is ordered in a way that makes them feel safe and secure."

For Liya, there is no distinction between responsible kink and kink. "If someone were to disregard mental health completely when it comes to kink, in my opinion, it's bordering on abuse." You can be really rough and vulgar and frankly, mean, in kink, and still consider the other person's mental health.

It's so important to discuss boundaries ahead of time because it's all about communication. If two people speak ahead of time, and it is clear that verbal degradation and insults are something that the submissive is comfortable with, and even aroused by, then that's a scenario where being really rough is still safe and responsible. But if someone is being a hard Dom/me with no remorse, and no prior communication, this can lead to lasting damage (and additional trauma) for that submissive. "That's not what I'm here for."

Why Femdom?

Liya says she has always been a very maternal and nurturing person to those she cares about. "Being able to explore that with a person that I trust and have a mutual respect for is a really beautiful thing. I think everyone should be able to experience that type of mutual understanding at least once."

Being a Domme has also helped her understand her own needs so much better, as well as what she expects from a relationship and what respect looks like to her.

"I think kink is so closely tied to emotional awareness. You need to be aware of your own needs while also looking out for the other person's needs completely."

Complete Obedience

Liya has a very specific type when it comes to subs. She

is a big fan of complete obedience. Although she says brats can be fun, she wants someone who is completely devoted. She enjoys general obedience training, servicing, complete devotion, and body worship. She's also a huge fan of feminization and total power exchange.

"I can be strict, but I'm not a sadist. I don't derive pleasure from hurting people. I only employ pain in play when punishment is needed"—slapping, spanking, and flogging, for example. She doesn't enjoy sadism for sadism's sake. That's why her hard limits are around unreasonable brutality and pain.

————————◇————————

"...kink is so closely tied to emotional awareness. You need to be aware of your own needs while also looking out for the other person's needs completely."
-Miss Liya

————————◇————————

Advice for New Dommes

Liya believes it is important for Dommes to enjoy what they do. If you are not a dominant individual in your personal life, you might not particularly enjoy having a submissive. This varies from person to person, however.

It is also important to be clear about your intentions upfront. When Liya tells people that she is a professional Domme, many respond that they want to be taught about it because they want the money. "But if you're only in it for the money, it's important to be upfront with the submissive about your disinterest in it."

You will find people who are into degradation enough to enjoy the humiliation of paying you despite your disliking them. "However, if you don't make those intentions clear, it can harm the rest of the community who is genuinely looking for that connection. And it can leave a bad taste in people's mouths."

How to Find a Domme

If you are looking to find a lifestyle Domme to be romantically involved and have a long-term relationship with (as opposed to a professional Domme where you pay for their services), Liya advises starting locally. You can use regular dating apps like Tinder or Bumble. "The trick is to put in specific, often subtle, keywords so people with like-minded interests can find you."

That's actually how Liya found her personal full-time submissive. He mentioned "mommy issues" in his bio. Most people wouldn't even notice it but to Liya, that was like a dog whistle, signaling that he has submissive inclinations.

Starting locally is so much more helpful than just searching widely online, according to Liya. You actually have a better chance of finding someone who is near you. "So many subs focus their energy on kink sites and apps, which is fine if you're okay with the relationship and interactions likely remaining online and not leading to a serious romantic endeavor."

Liya makes it clear to everyone she engages with online that she does not want any misconceptions about the nature of the relationship. She will train people online, but clearly tells them that she is not their girlfriend and they should not get their hopes up that their relationship will evolve beyond a professional nature.

Sadly, not all online Dommes have the courtesy to remind their subs of the reality of their dynamic. "A lot of people are just there because they are horny at the moment or just want to talk about fantasies, not making it clear that there is no interest in a relationship beyond the professional." This easily muddies the waters, leading to hurt feelings on the sub's behalf.

Boundaries Matter

Liya cautions submissives against Dominants who do not establish boundaries and needs early on. This can lead to really sticky scenarios down the line, like the sub finding themselves being blackmailed (without consenting to it).

"If you don't discuss your limits beforehand, these might later be misunderstood as someone acting bratty or disobedient rather than it being a hard boundary for someone and they're getting hurt."

Unfortunately, finding a romantic, personal femdom relationship online is difficult and rare. It can often lead subs to be taken advantage of by fake accounts posing as dominants.

―――――◇―――――

"If you don't discuss your limits beforehand, these might later be misunderstood as someone acting bratty or disobedient rather."
-Miss Liya

―――――◇―――――

Approaching a Professional Domme

Liya does not engage with the vast majority of DMs she gets online. She only responds if she is approached with respect, not with inappropriate remarks or requests. When approaching her, Liya advises that people start by introducing themselves, stating that they are aware of her being a professional Domme and that they are interested in learning under her.

She gets a lot of messages from submissives speaking only about what they want. "Although it's good to know what you are after, it's not good etiquette to make demands upfront when first approaching a professional Domme. It will likely not get you far."

Breaking the Stigma

Liya and her personal sub have been together for a year and a half. He understands the difference between their relationship and her professional interactions. For him, all that matters is that she is mentally his. He does not want to hear about her other sexual interactions at all but focuses on their personal relationship instead.

When in public together, most people assume that her submissive is the dominant one, which Liya finds very funny. He's 6'2", so everyone just makes assumptions. "Little do they know he ties my shoes for me and kisses my legs for forgiveness."

There is so much stigma around what a "man" should want or do. Liya has encountered submissives online who will block her and then come back a few weeks later, begging for forgiveness because they felt so ashamed of wanting to be submissive that they couldn't handle it and wanted to get rid of it completely.

"And it's really sad for me because I am pretty well aware of my dominance and I don't feel a lot of shame around it." But not everyone has done as much soul-searching as Liya to reach this point of acceptance. Often people feel the need to engage in kink but cannot separate this need from feelings of shame. They cannot even fully embrace their own identity or their sexual needs because they feel like they need to be the strong dominant one because of social pressures.

Liya's advice to those battling such social pressures is to find your people. The alternative crowd, for instance, is very accepting of femdom and even embraces it. "If you surround yourself with open-minded people who are emotionally aware, you'll find a way stronger support system than from the general public."

After all, this is a community.

Goddess Beatriz: Every Domme is Unique

Despite the limited representation of lifestyle Dommes in the media, Goddess Beatriz reminds us that Dommes are people too—complete with feelings, hobbies, and individual needs.

Discovering femdom has completely changed Goddess Beatriz's life. The 40-year-old US-based gentle Domme says it has been both empowering and a great confidence boost.

How did she get into the community and what advice does she have for beginners? Sex, shame, kink, and gender roles... Beatriz openly shares her insights.

An Instant Connection

While Beatriz currently has a long-distance submissive in Italy, she has also been dabbling in the local dating scene. She plans to meet up with her 31-year-old Italian play partner for the first time during an upcoming European trip. But for now, their dynamic has been a completely online experience.

Her submissive actually found her through Instagram and they hit it off from the get-go. She describes him as a "gentleman" who did all the right things when he initially approached her. He did not get straight into the Domme stuff. No, he asked about her interests first and got to know her better. Shortly after, they started engaging in regular voice and video calls. "I opened up to him because he knew how to approach me."

Beatriz was not looking for anything serious at the time but found herself growing fonder of her new sub. However, the lack of physical touch in a long-distance dynamic has turned out to be challenging. Beatriz says she is an extremely physical person—in fact, physical touch is both her and her sub's love language. (Her other love language is Acts of Service.) That's why she looks forward a great deal to finally meeting him in person.

Her sub is relatively new to the community and Beatriz has had to put in a lot of work to teach him the ropes. Luckily, their good chemistry made her more open to guiding him in the process. "If we didn't have that mental connection, I don't think I would have done that."

Discovering Gentle Femdom

Goddess Beatriz always knew she had a dominant side in her, even in her early 20s, but she did not know how to express it. Back then, she was heavily into the alternative scene and the clubs she frequented had BDSM shows and kink stuff playing in the background while people danced. That is when she became intrigued about the lifestyle. Unfortunately, the people she dated were never interested in exploring this side of her.

Her first Domme experience came in her late 20s. She met a submissive through a dating app—he was relatively inexperienced too. They started dating and playing together. He was the first person Beatriz ever pegged. "I loved it! I realized that's what I was meant to be. This is for me. It felt very freeing. It was as if something was missing and I finally realized what it was."

Femdom, paired with a recent spiritual awakening and a lot of personal work, has left Goddess Beatriz feeling more empowered and confident. "It feels like reclaiming my power. It has helped me become a stronger person and just a badass bitch."

————————◇————————

"It feels like reclaiming my power. It has helped me become a stronger person and just a badass bitch."
-Goddess Beatriz

————————◇————————

Personal Kinks

Goddess Beatriz considers herself a "gentle" Domme. She does not enjoy humiliation or harder kinks because it is simply not part of her personality, she says. "To me, gentle femdom is about watching out for your submissive and making sure they are feeling okay. Giving someone a safe space is very important to me."

Creating this safe space—where someone can feel comfortable being vulnerable and open, where they won't be judged—is key to Beatriz. That is why aftercare is non-negotiable for her. "Whether they are a new submissive or an experienced one, it's important to regularly check in with your partner to see how they are doing."

Beatriz enjoys pegging and also has a strong kink for sound—"auralism" as it is called. Being vocal and loud is important for her but is something that many men battle with initially. Men are not used to being encouraged to moan or make sounds during sexual play. She enjoys restraints and tying people up too.

Beatriz also has a cum kink and particularly enjoys it when her subs eat their own cum. That's something not all men are comfortable with and she respects that. Others have consensually agreed to try it and ended up liking it.

She does not like beating up people or anything involving

blood—that is too far for her personally. She does enjoy flogging and slapping though. Other than that, she does not like leaving marks (unless it is on their ass).

Kink & Mental Health Awareness

Nurturing comes naturally to Beatriz, and her background in professional psychology has made her a firm advocate of good mental health. She used to be a counselor and assistant therapist. "That part of my personality has allowed me to be a better Domme as I always want to ensure people feel heard and seen."

However, dealing with submissive men can also be a challenge. Often self-consciousness and the fear of being judged force their submissive nature into the closet. That was Beatriz's experience with the first sub she dated. When she first pegged him, he struggled a lot with the mental aspect of his role and had a breakdown because he was questioning himself and his identity. He thought he was mentally prepared for being pegged, but he was not.

A lot of men do not realize the mental and emotional work involved with being okay with a woman pegging you. "It's about more than someone tying you up and getting physical." That is why it is so important to also have someone guiding and supporting you through it, especially if you're new to being submissive. There is a lot of trust involved. "You can't be submissive to someone if you don't trust them."

Kinky play cannot be separated from mental health. If

someone is not mentally stable, or dealing with a lot of issues internally, "it can really fuck them up." That's why it is so important to always be honest with your partner about your mental health and triggers. For instance, some people might want to be humiliated but then not have the mental capacity to take it. "Being a caring and responsible Domme means being aware of your sub's mental health."

Sub-abuse is not uncommon. Sadly, many subs have spoken to Beatriz about instances where a Domme made them feel like they could not say no. She never wants her own subs to feel this way. "It's important to check in with your sub. Don't just make assumptions." She encourages her subs to establish their safe word and use it if and when they need to.

When a sub says they do not need a safe word, that is an immediate red flag for Beatriz. It is an important boundary, and she won't play with a sub who does not have one. Otherwise, she would have no way of ensuring they are okay.

"I would just rather be open and I expect the same from people."

———————◇———————

"Being a caring and responsible Domme means being aware of your sub's mental health."
-Goddess Beatriz

———————◇———————

Advice for Dommes

"Get to know yourself first," Beatriz advises. Even before playing with someone else, it is crucial to truly know who you are and what you are into.

Take note of things like aftercare and mental health, the aspects that are not always talked about as openly. One needs to understand the ethics of being a Domme. That is why doing research is so important.

If you're getting to know someone who could be a potential sub, Beatriz says to follow your gut and always be careful. "If you feel like something is off, it's probably off." Many people unfortunately do not trust their intuition.

Advice for Subs

To find a suitable lifestyle Domme partner, Beatriz recommends using local dating apps or FetLife. Instagram is also an option.

She cautions against so-called Dom/mes who immediately ask for money, or those who start to manipulate a sub-to-be without establishing a connection upfront. Even Dom/mes offering professional services should be clear upfront on the terms of engagement.

Beatriz advises subs to not immediately send photos either. You never know who you are sending them to, she says. "There needs to be consent and a connection first." At least some form of vetting is vital.

Video calls are a good way to verify who you're engaging with. Even a simple voice call could confirm a person's identity. "Be cautious. If something feels wrong, trust yourself."

Be respectful when you reach out to a Domme. "Dommes are people too and you want to get that connection." Do not assume they want pics or to see you naked from the get-go. Do not use honorifics either. No Mommy, Mistress, Goddess, or similar titles.

If you do send someone a message, do not expect a reply. Most Dommes simply will not reply. They do not owe you a reply. "Don't bark orders at a Domme. Something is wrong if you do that."

Another word of advice—do your research. "Find out what it's really like, what you really want." Do not just go to a Domme and ask them questions you could have Googled. Do not waste people's time.

Openly Kinky

Beatriz is very open on her dating app bios about being a Domme looking for a meaningful relationship. Sadly, there are still many creepy people who send her inappropriate messages. Other Dom/mes also regularly reach out to her, asking her to dominate them.

Beatriz notes how a lot of people who reach out to her

are people you'd never guess were submissive—people of authority like cops, for instance.

Most of Beatriz's friends know about her Domme life, although she can sense that some would prefer not to. "I often feel like there is a lot of judgment because of traditional gender roles, and many people feel like a woman's role is to be more submissive." For a long time, Beatriz didn't talk about her Domme-side at all because of the supposed shame and stigma attached to it.

Some people even told her that they do not think Dommes are real, that they are just women with "daddy issues." Some women shame it because they believe "a man should be a man." Many are threatened simply by the idea of femdom. But Beatriz does not believe there is any need to feel shame.

"A man can still be masculine and be submissive. There is nothing wrong with that. I don't think it makes you less of a person because you want to be submissive, regardless of gender."

Her family, however, does not know about her lifestyle. "They wouldn't understand."

———————◇———————

"A man can still be masculine and be submissive. There is nothing wrong with that."
-Goddess Beatriz

———————◇———————

Misconceptions About Dommes

A significant portion of femdom representation on the internet portrays Dommes as heartless. Beatriz feels this has created a big misconception of the community. "Maybe it's true that some Dommes are heartless, but many of us are quite caring actually. I am a huge romantic and I have feelings and hobbies like everyone else. Femdom is not as black and white as it's represented online."

Many people often expect a Domme to dress a certain way—leather with whips and chains so commonly seen online and in porn. "But not every Domme is going to dress like that." Beatriz likes wearing delicate lingerie, for instance—that does not make her any less of a Domme. Yet she still gets told that it is not what a "real Domme" wears.

There is sadly still a lot of gatekeeping in the community, and initially this made Beatriz very self-conscious because she liked wearing silky kimonos and bright colors too. That is why she was so happy to find alternative representations on social media which show Dommes dressing the way they want, each with their own style.

Dommes are people too, each with their unique style, personality, and list of preferred kinks. Remember this next time you try to fit them all into the same box.

A Queen + Her Knight: Ari Meets Mistress Nazz

Ari's been looking for his ideal Domme partner since his teenage years in the States—who knew he'd find her in Thailand?

Ari Chase-Ramos (32) is an up-and-coming author currently writing about his experiences of meeting his Queen—Mistress Nazz—in Thailand. The couple met on Tinder this year and have been playing together since, helping Mistress Nazz unlock a naturally dominant side she did not even know she had.

How did this unlikely duo find each other and what advice do they have for others seeking a gentle femdom lifestyle dynamic?

Unconventional Love Story

For Ari and Mistress Nazz, things happened quite quickly. After chatting for two weeks on Tinder, they agreed to meet up for dinner. Things started off as normal, vanilla dating, but both parties knew upfront that the other had kinky inclinations—this was already established before the first meeting.

This was Nazz's first venture into femdom—but not Ari's. He knew what he wanted and set up his dating profile accordingly, making it obvious that he sought a dominant partner. For example, his profile included a picture of him wearing a collar and another of Aristotle being ridden by a woman.

"I always knew I was submissive," Ari says. He discovered femdom in his teens already but was scared to delve deeper into his fantasies; he did not really know where to look for what he wanted. Over the years, he dated some girls who were open to certain parts of kinky play, but never anyone willing to commit to a full femdom dynamic. Not until he met Queen Nazz...

As Ari got older, especially during the pandemic, he started feeling freer to try different things and actually met a Domme in real life for the first time. Things did not work out though. Then, when he got to Thailand, he set up his Tinder to represent more accurately what he was looking for.

Shortly after, he matched with Nazz on the app. Their chat

went straight into kinky topics. Ari was immediately drawn to her wicked sense of humor and knew quite early on that had found who he was looking for.

These days, Nazz's close friends know about her dynamic with Ari and they are very supportive. "They know me and they can see that I'm happy." But her other friends often just feel weird when she openly starts talking about it. They do not want to know more. This is a common response and can be hard to deal with.

How Does It Work?

The couple is monogamous but does not practice their dynamic 24/7; they do not live together but spend a lot of time together. Although Nazz is dominant and likes to make decisions for both of them, Ari still retains his freedom to stand up for himself.

Nazz considers them a good match because Ari adjusts himself to match her energy—and she also adjusts to match him. It took some time to get to know each other and learn what they are into, but both were willing to put in the work—and actually enjoyed exploring. They still do.

It helps that Nazz is a quick learner. Even when trying certain kinky scenes for the first time, she quickly picked it up and got into it. To the point that she was soon coming up with ideas for role plays and scenarios herself. "I feel more fun when playing with Ari. It's because I trust him and I'm comfortable."

Ari likes that Nazz is open-minded and very funny. "And she takes care of me." He explains how their relationship has grown and how they have gotten more comfortable with each other over time. It is the little things she does that make him happy. Like buying food and feeding him.

Nazz says it is like having a pet. You love and feed them and cuddle and kiss them. "And if he's naughty or doesn't listen to me, I'll get mad and punish him." Although she is very nurturing, she can be quite a strict teacher too. Most importantly, "I enjoy being with him," Nazz says.

A few times they even displayed their dynamic in public with Nazz putting Ari on a leash and walking him through the markets or to the bar. "It was really cool how that developed because at first, I was like scared to do it, but I just did it," Ari says. "Some people were looking at us funny, but who cares?"

For Ari, getting rid of the shame that he personally felt for his desires has been a journey. "Now I'm at the point now where I just don't care what people think or how they see me." Often it's just you imagining how people would see you, making it worse in your head.

"We might pretend that she's torturing me or playing mean, but we really care about each other"
-Ari

Open to Explore

In terms of boundaries and the kinds of kinks they enjoy, the couple is pretty open and likes to explore new things together. Their hard limits lie in blood and permanent scarring.

Nazz particularly enjoys taking photos and humiliating Ari. She also likes dressing sexy, wearing something kinky like stockings and heels. Also gloves. And she enjoys putting Ari between her legs, she says.

There are still some scenes they haven't explored yet but are curious to try—like pegging. Ari has never been pegged but is open to the idea of Nazz pegging him in the future—when they're both ready.

The couple considers their dynamic a gentle femdom one. "We might pretend that she's torturing me or playing mean, but we really care about each other," Ari explains. "We're doing the scene because we're enacting some kind of fantasy. But I always know it's a fantasy, set in a certain time and space. It can always be ended if it goes too far or I get out of my headspace. I always feel very safe."

The couple has a safe word, so Ari knows he can always stop a scene if need be. Especially at first, Nazz did not know how far she could go. But now they know each other better and Ari has not had to use his safe word again in ages.

"It comes back to trusting your partner and knowing no real harm will come to you," Ari explains.

It's not just about keeping each other safe physically, but mentally too. There are a lot of emotions involved in a scene sometimes, a rollercoaster of emotions that can lead to sub-drop after a scene if not managed properly. But Ari has not experienced any sub-drop since playing with Nazz. He attributes this to knowing himself better and knowing how to handle a scene. The security he has in their dynamic also helps.

With a previous play partner, he didn't have a lot of boundaries and would say yes to almost anything. That, coupled with the insecurity of their relationship, led to some crazy sub-drop at the time, he remembers.

Now he has learned how to balance playing the slave while still standing up for himself, if it is needed. "I've realized that it's about going after what you and your partner both mutually want, not just trying to be the perfect slave and saying yes to everything." This is a balance many new subs struggle to find, often ignoring red flags and not setting any boundaries. "You don't really know when to stop at first. You're so excited to try it and it can lead to abuse if you're not careful."

The couple practices aftercare but does not really identify it as such. It just naturally forms part of their dynamic and how they look after and care for each other. For instance, a scene might start with Nazz making Ari worship her feet, or maybe whipping him or putting a candle on him. This leads to him licking her pussy and maybe even penetrative sex.

Afterwards, it naturally gets to the cuddling part.

Impact of Femdom

Femdom has had a big impact on Nazz's life. "It just makes me feel confident. And I never feel guilty. It's just fun and has fulfilled something in my life that I never had before."

Ari was not only Nazz's first femdom experience but also her first long-term relationship. She had only had short dating experiences before. "When I met Ari, I was a bit confused about whether I liked this way or not. But the more I got to know him, the more I realized I do enjoy playing like this. It's a part of my life now. He opened my mind."

According to Ari, even though Nazz had no previous femdom experience, from the moment they started talking, it was clear that she was completely dominant and "bossy." Even before meeting, she told him she was going to be his "devil Mistress" and make him sleep by her feet. "She was a natural right from the start."

Before moving to Thailand, Ari lived in China for several years. He spoke the local language fluently and dated local girls. They were only ever into certain parts of femdom and he never managed to experiment more and explore the other kinks he was into. For instance, the one girl only wanted to sit on his face and make him worship her pussy. "Now I get to try it all."

Ari was always drawn to the idea of service and wanted to

be the knight to his queen. Even when having vanilla sex or doing a simple position like missionary, the focus should still be on making her cum. "For me, it's about making sure that she's serviced and happy first."

———————◇———————

"Start slowly. Try not to kill each other. See what you both like and find the balance."
-Queen Nazz

———————◇———————

A Word of Advice

Nazz's advice to new Dommes is simple: "Start slowly. Try not to kill each other. See what you both like and find the balance." It takes time to get to know someone and find out where your (and their) limits lie. "Relationships take time. Don't rush things." Do research and get to know your partner.

It can be a struggle to find a true dominant partner, Ari added. His advice to subs seeking a femdom relationship is to first try to incorporate kinky play into a "normal" relationship and not to be shy to ask for what they want. This could be easier said than done though. "It goes against traditional gender roles, and many have shame around that and don't know how to bring it up."

But if you do not ask, you'll always end up wanting something, missing something, Ari says. "So in my experience, it's always best to start the conversation early. Find out if the girl you're pursuing is open to a potentially kinky dynamic."

Ari's key advice to subs can be summed up in one line: "Don't be an asshole." According to him, "a sub should be a gentleman"—especially when pursuing a dominant woman and wanting to serve her.

He also cautions against being a pushover. "Be open-minded and be flexible." Plus, be a good listener, and do not make it all about you—especially if you want to be put in a submissive role. Listen to what the Domme wants (and needs) too. "Be respectful."

When consuming online femdom content, be mindful of the context, Ari says. Know that you are consuming some made-up story that is engaging with your fantasies. Many of the portrayals show the extremes, often showing the Domme as sadistic or the villain (especially in Hollywood). "But that's not real life, that's fantasy."

There are some good movies though. Ari recommends a Korean movie called "Love & Leashes" (on Netflix), which follows two colleagues at work trying to find a relationship that suits them both. It really shows them encountering real problems that dominant women and submissive men encounter in their relationships in life. They are also very caring and supportive of each other.

---◇---

"Be respectful"
-Ari

---◇---

Telling Their Story

Ari feels very lucky that his Queen Nazz supports him and loves the fact that he consumes kinky content. She was the one who encouraged him to publish his first erotic novella—featuring the events of when they met and their story together.

After they played together, he wrote the first draft of the story in only 30 minutes on his phone. Nazz liked it so much that she told him to write a longer version. Ari did, and Nazz shared it with her friends. Everyone liked it and that's how his first novella Learning to Love My Leash came about... (*Check it out online if you want to know more.*)

TIPS FOR KINKSTERS

The following section contains summaries and extracts from the seven interviews conducted.

These are not the viewpoints of the author, nor are they shared as absolute facts. They are instead the personal insights of the individuals interviewed, based on their personal experiences. Take them as such and learn from them what you will.

For more information or to understand the context around the highlighted sections, refer back to the original interview articles.

Above all, be responsible, be kind.

TIPS FOR DOM/MES

Miss Kitty:

Being a Dom/me is a huge responsibility—do not take it lightly.

A good Dom/me, whether just a play-partner or in a loving relationship, is protective over their submissive.

A good dominant will support their submissive to be themselves, embracing their individuality.

Do not bully your submissive.

Respect your submissives and their boundaries.

Do not have set ideas about what your domination will look like from the get-go. This can change and evolve as you grow.

Be mindful that you're taking on a lot of responsibility for somebody's physical and emotional safety as a Dom/me. And if you're not willing to take on that responsibility in addition to the fun parts, maybe a sub-Dom/me dynamic isn't for you.

Research is key. If you cannot reach out to a local community, actual literature is the next best thing.

If you are not willing to do the work and wrap your head around how it works, then maybe BDSM is not for you.

Venus:

You have to make sure that both partners' needs are met, and the only way to do that is by communicating what your needs are. This type of dynamic does not work unless you are able to really communicate.

Do your research about anything and everything. If you are even mildly interested in something, do proper research to see how this can be safely and happily incorporated into your sex life.

When engaging with your sub, have an open discussion to ensure you have valid consent and they are comfortable with what is happening.

Don't push anything on your sub they are not comfortable with.

Understanding yourself and your own sexuality, and understanding that of your partner, is critical in crafting a healthy, happy, and sexy dynamic.

Treat your sub (if they're into it). Boys also deserve flowers—or maybe a cup of coffee if you wake up first. Just because they're your sub does not mean that you cannot do nice things for them.

Madam Mayhem:

Know that a Dom/me does not have to stick to one particular type of dominance. Kink is what you make it out to be, and you can customize it to suit you.

Figure out what you enjoy. Do not force yourself to be a certain kind of way based on the representations you see.

Do as much research as you can to improve your knowledge of femdom.

If you can, dive into your community. Kinksters are generally very open-minded and non-judgmental. They genuinely want to help you on your journey.

Be patient. Accept that kink is a lifetime journey. The more you get involved, the more you will discover. The more you discover, the more you will find new things you want to try.

Goddess Pinky:

As a dominant, you have to keep your submissive safe. Whether or not their needs seem silly to you, they are not silly. It's not your space to determine what their needs are for emotional health and physical safety.

Everyone has their own story with different traumas. You never know what will trigger someone.

Miss Liya:

It is important for Dom/mes to enjoy what they do.

Kink is so closely tied to emotional awareness. You need to be aware of your own needs, while also looking out for the other person's needs completely.

Be clear about your intentions upfront. If you are only in it for the money, it is important to be upfront with the submissive about your disinterest in it.

Goddess Beatriz

Get to know yourself first. Even before playing with someone else, it is key to truly know who you are and what you are into.

Take note of things like aftercare and mental health.

One needs to understand the ethics of being a Dom/me. That is why doing research is so important.

If you are getting to know someone who could be a potential sub, follow your gut and always be careful.

If you feel like something is off, it is probably off.

It's okay to be who you are. Many people often expect a Domme to dress a certain way—the leather, whips and chains so commonly seen online and in porn. But not every Domme is going to dress like that, nor do they have to.

Queen Nazz:

Start slowly. Try not to kill each other. See what you both like and find the balance.

It takes time to get to know someone and find out where your (and their) limits lie. Relationships take time. Do not rush things.

Do research and get to know your partner.

TIPS FOR SUBS

Miss Kitty:

Try to be more careful and less desperate.

You're allowed to say no. You do not have to do things you are not comfortable with to be a "good sub."

Know your power. A sub actually carries more control than the dominant. No matter how extreme a scene gets, the sub has a safe word, giving them ultimate control.

Watch out for fake Dom/mes. If they are trying to guilt trip or manipulate you into doing something you genuinely don't want to do, and you've communicated why you do not want to, then they are not a genuine Dom/me.

Trust your instincts. If something's giving you a red flag, it is a red flag.

If you want to make use of a professional service, make sure they are legit first.

Venus:

Do your research to find out what you are into and what you want. The more you understand yourself, the better you will be able to bring this up to your partner in an open-minded way.

Just because you are a sub doesn't mean that you cannot be involved in some of the decision-making processes of what you do in the dynamic.

Recognize your power. No matter what happens in a scene, the sub has the power to stop it with their safe word/s.

Do not just go in assuming that any Dom/me is going to be just perfect for you. That is not how it works. There needs to be compatibility.

Do not just fixate on the sexual part—there is so much more to gentle femdom. Without emotional intimacy, the sexual part is not even half as fulfilling.

Trusting your partner is key to ensuring a good experience for both.

Mayhem:

Don't just throw yourself into the kinky world uninformed. Familiarize yourself with the ideas of aftercare and consent.

Learn about Risk-Aware/ Accepted Consensual Kink (RACK) and other good practices so that you can spot the fakes.

If you want to be pegged, test the waters first. Use a toy on yourself (like a buttplug) and find out if it is the feeling you enjoy and not just the idea.

By exploring on their own first, a sub will know more about their own pleasure and limits by the time they play with a partner.

Do not try to force a connection. If the chemistry is not there, you cannot fake it.

Goddess Pinky:

Highlight your non-negotiable requirements to your dominant partner(s).

If you are not okay after a scene, say so.

Ensure a clear understanding of safe words and boundaries upfront.

Miss Liya:

Be cautious of Dominants who do not establish boundaries and needs early on. This can lead to really sticky scenarios down the line, like the sub finding themselves being blackmailed (without consenting to it).

If you do not discuss your limits beforehand, these might later be misunderstood as someone acting bratty or disobedient rather than being hard boundaries for someone and they are getting hurt.

Be wary of so-called Dom/mes who immediately ask for money, or those who start to manipulate a sub-to-be without establishing a connection upfront.

Goddess Beatriz

Do not immediately send photos when talking to a new Dom/me online. You never know who you are sending them to. There needs to be consent and a connection first.

At least some form of vetting is vital.

Video calls are a good way to verify who you are engaging with. Even a simple voice call could confirm a person's identity.

Be cautious. If something feels wrong, trust yourself.

Do your research. Find out what it's really like, what you really want. Do not just go to a Dom/me and ask them questions you could have Googled. Do not waste people's time.

Ari the sub:

Do not be shy to ask for what you want. If you do not ask, you will always end up wanting something, missing something.

Do not be an asshole.

A sub should be a gentleman—especially when pursuing a dominant woman and wanting to serve her.

Do not be a pushover. But be open-minded and be flexible.

Be a good listener, and do not make it all about you—especially if you want to be put in a submissive role. Listen to what the Domme wants (and needs) too.

Be respectful.

When consuming online femdom content, be mindful of the context. Know that you are consuming some made-up story that is engaging with your fantasies.

Go after what you and your partner both mutually want. Do not just try to be the perfect slave and say yes to everything.

Responsible Kink + Mental Health

Miss Kitty:

There is more to being a Dom/me than just having sex and giving orders.

As the dominant, you are the caretaker of your submissive and their emotional health and well-being within that dynamic.

Be wary of online dynamics where the sub (or Dom/me) is not properly supported. There is much more to a Dom/me-sub dynamic than what you see in pornography.

Being put into a submissive state can lead to a lot of emotions for a sub and it is important for a Dom/me to support them through this.

It's important to ensure both parties' needs are met in the dynamic.

The biggest danger with online representation is the unsafe extremes portrayed. It's dangerous because it makes it look like anybody could do it with the right mindset. Yet there is little to no representation of how to do things safely.

BDSM is not an excuse to be a bad person.

Coercive control is a form of domestic abuse. Often people try and wrap a bow on controlling, manipulative behavior and call it BSDM. But it is not BDSM, you are just a bad partner—no matter what type of relationship you enter.

Madam Mayhem:

Provide a safe space for subs to indulge their submissive tendencies, to allow them the freedom of such a release. Do not do that for someone unless you can always put their mental health first.

Goddess Pinky:

The real life of living this way is not the fantasy that we have online. It's much more complicated.

There are a lot of emotional things that surface and really vulnerable conversations that have to take place in order to have a healthy relationship when you like to be consensually physically abused.

If the idea of consent scares someone off, you do not want them in your life.

You do not want to really hurt someone. And if you do, that's not consensual kink.

No one's signing up for unbearable mental trauma. This should be a space for healing, not for making new wounds. This is not a space for abuse.

Safe spaces are very important.

Kink is supposed to be a safe space to explore things that you cannot explore in any other realm.

Even if it is a paid exchange for sex work, you should leave feeling like you received what you came for, not feeling traumatized by the experience.

Kink should be used to create healing experiences rather than traumatic ones.

Too often dominance and submission are painted as trauma-creating spaces, but for most, it is a way to reclaim something.

It is important that partners give informed consent. If subs are not capable of doing so, the dominant partner(s) should start slowly, especially with inexperienced subs who do not yet know their limits. You do not want to unintentionally assault someone.

Due diligence is key to avoiding hurting yourself or someone else.

If you are falling into the abuse cycle because you are in this lifestyle, you need to stop and reevaluate and renegotiate boundaries.

Do not go chasing erotic scenes you see online. Most of these scenes are staged, simply offering a highlight of a real engagement. There is so much more that goes on behind the scenes to ensure everyone's safety—physically and emotionally.

We have a responsibility to leave each other either the same or better than we found them. Otherwise, you're doing damage and no one wants that done to them.

Things like breath play and waterboarding can be very dangerous even when you know what you're doing. Start slow—do not immediately attempt the most extreme level.

When tying someone up, do not tie their hands at first. Build trust, then tie more.

Liya:

If someone disregards mental health completely when it comes to kink, it is bordering on abuse.

You can be really rough and vulgar, and frankly mean, in kink, and still consider the other person's mental health.

It's so important to discuss boundaries ahead of time because it is all about communication.

If two people speak ahead of time, and it's clear that

verbal degradation and insults are something that the submissive is comfortable with, and even aroused by, then that's a scenario where being really rough is still safe and responsible.

If someone is being a hard Dom/me with no remorse, and no prior communication, this can lead to lasting damage (and additional trauma) for that submissive.

Goddess Beatriz:

Gentle femdom is about watching out for your submissive and making sure they are feeling okay. Giving someone a safe space is very important.

A lot of men do not realize the mental and emotional work involved with being okay with a woman pegging you. It's about more than someone tying you up and getting physical.

Kinky play cannot be separated from mental health. If someone is not mentally stable, or dealing with a lot of issues internally, kinky play can really fuck them up.

It is important to always be honest with your partner about your mental health and triggers.

Being a caring and responsible Domme means being aware of your sub's mental health.

Sub-abuse is not uncommon. Many subs speak about instances where a Domme made them feel like they couldn't say no. Never make your subs feel this way.

It is important to check in with your sub. Do not just make assumptions.

Ari, the sub:

It is not just about keeping each other safe physically, but mentally as well.

There are a lot of emotions involved in a scene sometimes; a rollercoaster of emotions that can lead to sub-drop after a scene if not managed properly. Knowing oneself better and knowing how to handle a scene can help avoid this.

Safe Words + After Care

Miss Kitty:

A sub actually carries more control than the dominant. As a Dom/me, judge your sub's limits and what they're willing to do or not do. But at the end of the day, no matter how extreme you get, the sub has a safe word, giving them ultimate control.

If a Dom/me says you do not need a safe word, get away from that person—it is a massive red flag.

Madam Mayhem:

Aftercare negotiation is very important; it is key for making sure the submissive feels safe. They are trusting you and you would never want to breach that trust because being submissive is such a vulnerable state.

Be mindful of the often-overlooked Dom/me-drop. Subs are not the only ones who potentially have to deal with intense emotions after a scene.

Aftercare is important for *all* partners involved.

Goddess Pinky:

You need to ensure a clear understanding of safe words and boundaries upfront. While it is the dominant's responsibility to raise this, the submissive person has to have the emotional capacity to speak to their own limits and to stand firm in them. Or else you should not play with them.

Only physically hurt someone if they want you to. But you need to know that they understand how safe words work and that you are on the same page first.

Experience in the submissive role can offer understanding about the connection a sub has with their dominant partner—and how important aftercare and being valued is. Neglecting aftercare or gratitude can lead to a lot of drama.

You can be really mean—consensually. But you will feel like shit about it unless there's a way to reset the balance afterward (which differs from person to person). This is where aftercare comes in and having honest, open, and vulnerable conversations.

Do not engage in kinky play with someone if there is not a

way to restore balance before transitioning back into the real world.

You have to keep yourself safe. That's why things like the stoplight safe word system and the proper vetting partners are so important.

Goddess Beatriz:

Creating this safe space—where someone can feel comfortable being vulnerable and open, where they will not be judged—is key. That is why aftercare is non-negotiable.

Whether they are a new submissive or an experienced one, it is important to regularly check in with your partner to see how they are doing.

When a sub says they do not need a safe word, that's an immediate red flag. It is an important boundary and you should not play with a sub who does not have one. Otherwise, you have no way of ensuring they are okay.

Ari, the sub:

A couple might pretend that the dominant is torturing or playing mean with the sub, but it is important that they really care about each other.

Have a safe word, so that the sub knows they can always stop a scene if need be. Especially at first, the dominant might not know how far they can go. It comes back to trusting your partner and knowing no real harm will come to you.

Aftercare can naturally form part of a couple's dynamic and how they look after and care for each other—such as cuddling after a scene.

SOCIAL CONSTRUCTS + SHAME

Madam Mayhem:

The taboo around anything anal for cis-gendered heterosexual men is a big challenge.

Many men think that if they can find a woman to peg them, the act of enjoying anal pleasure won't be frowned upon as much by society. This can lead to potentially risky encounters with fake Dom/mes.

There is a bit of common sense involved that most men don't think about. They just think about the end goal and what they want, forgetting to educate themselves and to be patient until they find the right person.

Goddess Pinky:

Submissives, especially men, will often claim to be fine after a scene despite feeling the opposite. Perhaps male submissives do not always have the emotional language or awareness to say, 'Hey, I'm feeling down right now.'

Society dictates that men must not show weakness, which can make it even harder for them to identify and express their feelings.

Women are told to choke down their feelings and hide them in a room. But at least they are taught to understand them. Men are often literally physically abused for showing emotion as boys. And it really fucks them up.

Men should learn to drop the defensiveness over masculinity and realize it is not about hating men. It is about trying to fix the problem.

Men themselves are not the problem. It is the systems that we all subscribe to that have caused the problem.

The fact that this lifestyle is so taboo makes it very hard for the right people to meet up because everyone's trying to hide it. They do not know what to ask for—especially men living in more repressed societies. Often it makes people act crazy and causes a lot of assault and shame.

Shame has no place in sex. There should be no shame in our bodies or in wanting to have sex. There is shame in misusing people as objects, though. Not consensual objectification, but rather when people try to consume possessing others.

Just because you are kinky does not mean you cannot have a good relationship with your God.

Liya:

When in public together, people often make the wrong assumptions about who the submissive and dominant partners are, which can be very funny.

There is so much stigma around what a "man" should want or do, and this is reflected in some behavior online.

Some submissives block feel so ashamed of wanting to be submissive that they could not handle it and wanted to get rid of it completely. This can result in subs blocking Dom/mes they speak to online, only to return later and beg for forgiveness.

Not everyone has done the kind of soul-searching required to reach a point of acceptance. Often people feel the need to engage in kink but cannot separate this need from feelings of shame. They cannot even fully embrace their own identity or their sexual needs because they feel like they need to be the strong dominant one because of social pressures.

Miss Liya:

If you are battling social pressures to fit in, find your people. The alternative crowd, for instance, is very accepting of femdom and even embraces it.

If you surround yourself with open-minded people who are emotionally aware, you will find a way stronger support system than from the general public.

Goddess Beatriz:

There is a lot of judgment because of traditional gender roles and many people feel like a woman's role is to be more submissive. This means that some cannot talk about their Domme-side at all because of the supposed shame and stigma attached to it.

There is a misconception that Dommes are not real—that they're just women with daddy issues. Some women shame it because they believe "a man should be a man." Many are threatened simply by the idea of femdom.

A man can still be masculine and be submissive. There is nothing wrong with that.

It does not make you less of a person because you want to be submissive, regardless of gender.

FINDING A KINKY PARTNER

Miss Kitty:

Check out local heavy metal and alternative clubs. These people are generally more open-minded and can be a very supportive community.

You can also drop kinky comments into normal conversation jokingly (even at work) to test the waters and see who reacts.

Miss Liya:

If you are looking to find a lifestyle Dom/me to be romantically involved with and have a long-term relationship with (as opposed to a professional Dom/me where you pay for their services), start locally.

You can use regular dating apps like Tinder or Bumble.

The trick is to put in specific, often subtle, keywords so people with like-minded interests can find you. (Liya found her personal full-time submissive because he mentioned "mommy issues" in his bio.)

Starting locally is so much more helpful than just searching wide online. You actually have a better chance of finding someone who is near you.

So many subs focus their energy on kink sites and apps, which is fine if you're okay with the relationship and interactions likely remaining online and not leading to a serious romantic endeavor.

Goddess Beatriz:

To find a suitable lifestyle Dom/me partner, use local dating apps or FetLife.

Instagram is also an option.

Ari, the sub:

Set your dating profile up to reflect what you want, making it obvious that you are seeking a dominant partner. (For example, Ari's profile included a picture of him wearing a collar and one of Aristotle being ridden by a woman.)

If you match with someone on a dating app, start the conversation around your kinky needs early on. Find out if the girl you're pursuing is open to a potentially kinky dynamic.

How to Approach a Domme

Miss Kitty:

Instead of reaching out to people and saying like, 'Oh, can I be submissive' or 'can I call you Miss,' reach out to people to learn.

If someone is automatically trying to put you in a submissive role when you start chatting to them, they are not a proper Dom/me.

You are only their submissive if you are formally submitting to that individual Dom/me.

The same goes for people automatically call Dommes "Miss." The Domme has not consented to being your Miss.

If you message a potential Dom/me to ask for advice and

they immediately insist on you calling them by a title, or they want to put you in a submissive place from the start, that is not a proper Dom/me.

Be particularly wary when these people get defensive if you ask questions.

Venus:

It is very off-putting if a stranger address you by a title like "Miss" or "Mistress."

When chatting to people online or just in general—be an actual person.

Do not just try and force people into the role of Dom/me or sub.

Until you are actually in a dynamic, you cannot just call someone "Mistress"—it is rude and disrespectful.

Do not make it all about you when messaging someone. The Dom/me is not just there to provide a service for you. If you are paying them for it, then it is different. But if that is not what you are doing, then do not use them.

Do not see a Dom/me as just a vehicle for your own pleasure.

Madam Mayhem:

People who slide into a Domme's DMs and call them

"Mommy" off the bat do not recognize that there is a human being on the other side of that chat and that they have to treat them with respect.

Do not just immediately assume a Domme is going to do your bidding.

It boils down to being a decent human being, being respectful, and adhering to social norms when reaching out to a complete stranger.

Just do not be creepy.

Do not be rude.

That person does not owe you anything—especially not their valuable time and energy.

Miss Liya:

Dom/mes may not respond to the vast majority of DMs they get online. Do not expect them to.

When approaching a professional Dom/me online, start by introducing yourself and state that you are aware of them being a professional and that you are interested in learning under them.

As a submissive, do not just send messages describing what you want. Although it is good to know what you are after, it is not good etiquette to make demands upfront when first approaching a professional Dom/me. It will likely not get you far.

Goddess Beatriz:

Be respectful when you reach out to a Dom/me. Dom/mes are people too and you want to get that connection.

Do not assume they want pics or to see you naked from the get-go.

Do not use honorifics without permission either. No "Mommy," "Mistress," "Goddess," or similar titles.

If you do send someone a message, do not expect a reply. Most Dom/mes simply will not reply. They do not owe you a reply.

Do not bark orders at a Dom/me.

Ari, the sub:

Do not be an asshole. A sub should be a gentleman—especially when pursuing a dominant woman and wanting to serve her.

Sign-up to my monthly newsletter for more femdom stories and updates.

THANK YOU

Thank you for reading my book.

If you enjoyed it, won't you please take a moment to leave a review at your favorite retailer? It helps more like-minded people find this very niche content. Thank you!

Do you want additional gentle femdom content?

Then carry on reading...

M KAY NOIR

About M Kay Noir

M Kay Noir (36) is a South African journalist, author, and creator.

Noir has been a journalist for around 20 years, 17 of which overlap with writing erotic stories in one form or another. From school newspapers to international magazine editor, Noir has been writing and interviewing since a young teenager, building a career in reporting on sustainability and engineering matters.

These days, Noir has made it her mission to bring kindness and compassion to femdom erotica and romance, with a particular focus on gentle femdom. To improve the representation of realistic and healthy gentle femdom relationships, she started the Gentle Femdom Diaries interview series at the end of 2022.

MORE BY M KAY NOIR

House of Subs (Vol 1-4), *A Gentle Femdom Collection*

Want to explore gentle femdom fantasies in a safe space?
Introducing a fictional gentle femdom love story full of intimate moments and explicit scenes.

Follow Mistress Kay and Avi's kinky exploration as she teaches him how to be a good sub and an even better partner. A wholesome tale of love, sex, and kink.

Expect lots of sex. In every single one of the 74 chapters.

Not a traditional novel but rather a collection of web serial chapters, often standalone, featuring the same characters.

Available in paperback and ebook.

Connect with Me

Feel free to join my various online communities. I am most active on Instagram and Facebook, with TikTok growing quickly too. The best way to stay in the know, however, is to sign up for my monthly newsletter (mkaynoir.com/newsletter).

Most of my work is romance or erotica and as such, so are most of my posts. Representation matters and I want to represent beautiful, healthy kinky relationships where societal norms and gender roles are turned upside down. I particularly enjoy creating inclusive and queer content.

Find direct links via mkaynoir.com or email me for any info: mkay@mkaynoir.com

CONNECT WITH ME